CHANGING DEMANDS AND WATER SUPPLY UNCERTAINTY IN CALIFORNIA

OVERSIGHT HEARING

BEFORE THE

SUBCOMMITTEE ON WATER, POWER AND OCEANS

OF THE

COMMITTEE ON NATURAL RESOURCES
U.S. HOUSE OF REPRESENTATIVES

ONE HUNDRED FOURTEENTH CONGRESS

SECOND SESSION

Tuesday, July 12, 2016

Serial No. 114–49

Printed for the use of the Committee on Natural Resources

Available via the World Wide Web: http://www.fdsys.gov
or
Committee address: http://naturalresources.house.gov

U.S. GOVERNMENT PUBLISHING OFFICE

20–918 PDF   WASHINGTON : 2016

For sale by the Superintendent of Documents, U.S. Government Publishing Office
Internet: bookstore.gpo.gov   Phone: toll free (866) 512–1800; DC area (202) 512–1800
Fax: (202) 512–2104   Mail: Stop IDCC, Washington, DC 20402–0001

COMMITTEE ON NATURAL RESOURCES

ROB BISHOP, UT, *Chairman*
RAÚL M. GRIJALVA, AZ, *Ranking Democratic Member*

Don Young, AK
Louie Gohmert, TX
Doug Lamborn, CO
Robert J. Wittman, VA
John Fleming, LA
Tom McClintock, CA
Glenn Thompson, PA
Cynthia M. Lummis, WY
Dan Benishek, MI
Jeff Duncan, SC
Paul A. Gosar, AZ
Raúl R. Labrador, ID
Doug LaMalfa, CA
Jeff Denham, CA
Paul Cook, CA
Bruce Westerman, AR
Garret Graves, LA
Dan Newhouse, WA
Ryan K. Zinke, MT
Jody B. Hice, GA
Aumua Amata Coleman Radewagen, AS
Thomas MacArthur, NJ
Alexander X. Mooney, WV
Cresent Hardy, NV
Darin LaHood, IL

Grace F. Napolitano, CA
Madeleine Z. Bordallo, GU
Jim Costa, CA
Gregorio Kilili Camacho Sablan, CNMI
Niki Tsongas, MA
Pedro R. Pierluisi, PR
Jared Huffman, CA
Raul Ruiz, CA
Alan S. Lowenthal, CA
Matt Cartwright, PA
Donald S. Beyer, Jr., VA
Norma J. Torres, CA
Debbie Dingell, MI
Ruben Gallego, AZ
Lois Capps, CA
Jared Polis, CO
Wm. Lacy Clay, MO

Jason Knox, *Chief of Staff*
Lisa Pittman, *Chief Counsel*
David Watkins, *Democratic Staff Director*
Sarah Lim, *Democratic Chief Counsel*

———

SUBCOMMITTEE ON WATER, POWER AND OCEANS

JOHN FLEMING, LA, *Chairman*
JARED HUFFMAN, CA, *Ranking Democratic Member*

Don Young, AK
Robert J. Wittman, VA
Tom McClintock, CA
Cynthia M. Lummis, WY
Jeff Duncan, SC
Paul A. Gosar, AZ
Doug LaMalfa, CA
Jeff Denham, CA
Garret Graves, LA
Dan Newhouse, WA
Thomas MacArthur, NJ
Rob Bishop, UT, *ex officio*

Grace F. Napolitano, CA
Jim Costa, CA
Ruben Gallego, AZ
Madeleine Z. Bordallo, GU
Gregorio Kilili Camacho Sablan, CNMI
Raul Ruiz, CA
Alan S. Lowenthal, CA
Norma J. Torres, CA
Debbie Dingell, MI
Raúl M. Grijalva, AZ, *ex officio*

———

CONTENTS

OVERSIGHT HEARING ON CHANGING DEMANDS AND WATER SUPPLY UNCERTAINTY IN CALIFORNIA

Tuesday, July 12, 2016
U.S. House of Representatives
Subcommittee on Water, Power and Oceans
Committee on Natural Resources
Washington, DC

The subcommittee met, pursuant to call, at 10:02 a.m., in room 1324, Longworth House Office Building, Hon. John Fleming [Chairman of the Subcommittee] presiding.

Present: Representatives Fleming, Gosar, McClintock, Lummis, LaMalfa, Denham, Newhouse, Bishop (ex officio), Huffman, Costa, Ruiz, and Torres.

Dr. FLEMING. The Subcommittee on Water, Power and Oceans will come to order.

The Water, Power and Oceans Subcommittee meets today to hear testimony on an oversight hearing entitled Changing Demands and Water Supply Uncertainty in California. We will start with opening statements, beginning with myself.

STATEMENT OF THE HON. JOHN FLEMING, A REPRESENTATIVE IN CONGRESS FROM THE STATE OF LOUISIANA

Dr. FLEMING. Today's hearing is about fostering government accountability and restoring balance to a region devastated by natural and man-made drought. Achieving these objectives will help give the Federal Government the metrics to improve our environment, while allowing California's farmers to provide food and fiber to our Nation and the world.

This subcommittee is all too familiar with the historic drought that has impacted California. While there are various estimates of job losses, no one can disagree that number is in the thousands. With California providing the vast majority of fruits, nuts, and vegetables to grocery stores and tables nationwide, the drought has impacted all of us. With this year's El Niño, things were finally looking better for California. Many reservoirs are at historic capacity and farmers can use their water allocations as collateral for financing their planting season.

There are continued disappointments, however, as evidenced by the chart on the TV screen, which compares outflows to the ocean from this year to the last. It basically says that 350 percent more water flowed through the Delta so far this year, but that water users in Southern California were only allowed to capture 50 percent more than last year. As a result, they only have 5 percent of their water allocation.

Despite some general improvements, the U.S. Fish and Wildlife Service and the National Marine Fisheries Service have done their best to, as one of our water witnesses will say, "pull the rug out from under our feet" with proposed Federal regulations. These additional bites at the apple contradict what another arm of the Federal Government, the Bureau of Reclamation, has provided in the form of water allocations. This proves two things: what one Federal agency gives, another can take away; and Federal agencies are not communicating with each other, a recurring theme under this and prior administrations.

What makes matters worse is that many are charging that the proposed fish flows were not based on scientific justification or peer review. Once again, the so-called most transparent administration in history is anything but. I am not aware of anyone who wants to see a species go extinct, but Federal actions need to be justified and have tangible goals. As we will hear later, the proposed flows for these 3-inch Delta smelt lack any controls or metrics to measure the results of the action and lack any impact analysis on water users, refuges, and other fish and wildlife needs.

To add insult to injury, these proposed Delta smelt flows are to the detriment of the salmon flows. Of course, fish need water, but real science, not political science in this case, should dictate how much water a species needs.

These agencies also need to be communicating with communities who depend on water from the same system. Instead, the proposals took most of the communities by surprise and continue to put a cloud over water supplies in parts of California.

While the focus of today is on California, this is a case study of Federal unaccountability and confusion that could be imposed anywhere else in the Nation. This hearing is part of an effort to provide a blueprint for Federal transparency in order to avoid further man-made issues. The Federal Government can clearly do better, although the bar is pretty low in this case.

We have before us experts who understand these matters firsthand. I thank them for traveling here. I also want to thank our colleague, Mr. LaMalfa, for asking for this hearing.

I now recognize the Ranking Member, Mr. Huffman, for his statement.

[The prepared statement of Mr. Fleming follows:]

PREPARED STATEMENT OF THE HON. JOHN FLEMING, CHAIRMAN, SUBCOMMITTEE ON WATER, POWER AND OCEANS

Today's hearing is about fostering government accountability and restoring balance to a region devastated by natural and man-made drought. Achieving these objectives will help give the Federal Government the metrics to improve our environment while allowing California's farmers to provide food and fiber to our Nation and the world.

This subcommittee is all too familiar with the historic drought that has impacted California. While there are various estimates of job losses, no one can disagree that they number in the thousands. With California providing the vast majority of fruits, nuts and vegetables to grocery stores and tables nationwide, the drought has impacted all of us.

With this year's El Niño, things were finally looking better for California. Many reservoirs are at historic capacity and farmers can use their water allocations as collateral for financing the planting season. There are continued disappointments, however, as evidenced by the chart on the screen (see below), which compares outflows to the ocean from this year to the last. It basically says that 350 percent more water flowed through the Delta so far this year, but that water users south of there were only allowed to capture 50 percent more than last year. As a result, they only have 5 percent of their water allocation.

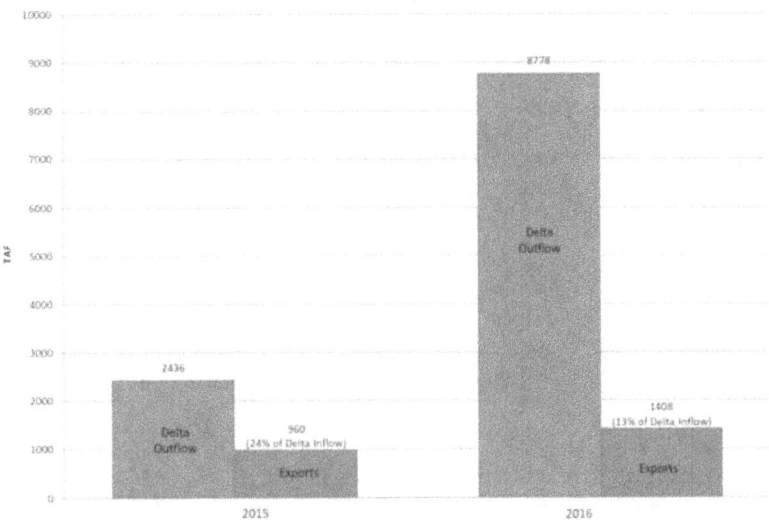

Delta Outflow and Export
2015 vs 2016 (Jan1-Jun30)

Source: San Luis & Delta-Mendota Water Authority

Despite some general improvements, the U.S. Fish and Wildlife Service and the National Marine Fisheries Service have done their best to, as one of our water witnesses will say, "pull the rug out from under our feet" with proposed Federal regulations. These additional bites at the apple run contrary to what another arm of the Federal Government—the Bureau of Reclamation—has provided in the form of water allocations. This proves two things: what the Federal Government gives, it can certainly take away; and Federal agencies are once again contradicting each other, a recurring theme under this and prior administrations.

What makes matters worse is that many are charging that the proposed fish flows were not based on scientific justification or peer review. Once again, the so-called most transparent administration in history is anything but. I'm not aware of anyone who wants to see a species go extinct, but Federal actions need to be justified and have tangible goals. As we will hear later, the proposed flows for the 3-inch Delta smelt lack any controls or metrics to measure the results of the action and lack any impact analysis on water users, refuges, and other fish and wildlife needs. To add insult to injury, these proposed Delta smelt flows would have been contrary to the salmon flows. Of course fish need water, but real science—not political science in this case—should dictate how much water a species needs.

And there needs to be prior conversation with the communities who depend on water from the same system. Instead, the proposals took most communities by surprise and continue to put a cloud over water supplies in parts of California.

While the focus of today is on California, it is a case study of Federal unaccountability and confusion that could be imposed anywhere else in the Nation. This hearing is part of an effort to provide a blueprint for Federal transparency in order to avoid further man-made issues.

The Federal Government can clearly do better, although the bar is pretty low in this case. We have before us experts who understand these matters firsthand. I thank them for traveling here and I also want to thank our colleague, Mr. LaMalfa, for asking for this hearing.

STATEMENT OF THE HON. JARED HUFFMAN, A REPRESENTATIVE IN CONGRESS FROM THE STATE OF CALIFORNIA

Mr. HUFFMAN. Thank you, Mr. Chairman.

I want to welcome the witnesses, especially my constituent, Mr. Borck, who has come a long way from Humboldt County, California.

This is the last week, Mr. Chairman, that we are here before heading back to our districts for 7 weeks. I think it is important to point out that when we return, we will have only 8 weeks left in this Congress. There are a number of very important issues that we ought to be addressing; unfortunately, we are here once again in this subcommittee wasting taxpayer dollars on a farce of a hearing to attack the Endangered Species Act and blame environmental protections for California's drought, even though this preposterous claim has been debunked time and again. But I guess I really shouldn't be surprised.

The standard bearer right now for the Republican party, Donald Trump, famously said a few weeks ago in California's Central Valley that there is no drought. He went on to make the same claims that we are going to hear today, blaming water shortages on the Endangered Species Act. His statement on California's drought was rightfully mocked by experts, found to be false by nonpartisan, independent fact checkers, and yet apparently that fact checking did not sink in here in this Congress.

So, let me share a few facts. Fact one, the 2014 water year was the third driest in recorded history, and according to experts, paleontologists, folks who study tree ring records, they conclude the current drought in California is likely the most severe in 1,200 years. According to the U.S. Drought Monitor, 100 percent of the state is currently experiencing some level of drought. To say there is no hydrological drought in California is absurd.

Another fact, the Department of the Interior estimates that the Endangered Species Act accounted for a mere 2 percent of the water supply reduction in the Central Valley Project (CVP) water deliveries in the year 2014 and similar small impacts in 2015. In other words, if there was no Endangered Species Act, if my Republican colleagues got everything they want, simply eliminated the Endangered Species Act, they would get about 2 percent more water in the year 2014, maybe a little bit more than that in 2015.

Third fact, California's State Water Board estimated that in 2015, of all the runoff in the Bay Delta watershed that flowed to San Francisco Bay, in other words, the water that Donald Trump says was being "shoved to the sea by environmentalists," only 2 percent of this runoff actually flowed out to the ocean solely for environmental protection. The vast majority was released to keep the system from salting up, for salinity control, so that we could continue to have that water used by agriculture, by cities, by millions of people who depend on it.

While we are in fact check mode, I want to also examine this notion that somehow California's farming industry is not getting water because of the Endangered Species Act. While some people with vested interests continue to peddle this fiction, the numbers tell a different story. Even in this fifth year of a historic drought, millions of acre-feet of water are being delivered to major agricultural water users. For example, one of the Republican witnesses today, the Tehama-Colusa Canal Authority, will get 100 percent of its maximum water allocation this year. The other Republican witness represents a large group of Ag. users in the San Joaquin Valley that includes the San Joaquin Valley exchange contractors, and they are projected to get 100 percent of their maximum water allocation of around 800,000 acre-feet, for free by the way.

So, make no mistake, Mr. Chairman, a tremendous amount of water is being delivered to agriculture during this drought. In fact, if you average together all the CVP deliveries for all the different contractors, most of whom are agricultural water users, the CVP is expected to deliver about 60 percent of maximum contract quantities this year.

Now, some junior contractors will be significantly impacted much more than those that are getting 100 percent or those that are getting high allocations. That is because they have no water rights, that is because that is the way the system works. But it does not mean they will have no water, because they will buy water from some of those that are getting the high allocations, they will turn to other sources, and they will have some water, even though there will be sacrifice, as you would expect in the fifth year of a critical drought.

It is true that much of the water has been made available, and this is an important point because year after year state and Federal agencies have taken water that was supposed to be used to sustain California's fisheries and they have redirected it, primarily to powerful agricultural interests. Fisheries protections have been cut to the bone and the result has been a disaster for salmon fishermen. There is a zero buffer for endangered fish in this drought.

Federal officials recently announced that there was a 97 percent mortality rate for juvenile Sacramento River winter-run salmon in 2015. The year before that it was 95 percent mortality. So, there is extreme hardship for the families, communities, and tribes who depend on salmon. There are jobs on the ecosystem side of this water system as well, and that is something that we will continue to point out.

Thank you, Mr. Chairman.

[The prepared statement of Mr. Huffman follows:]

PREPARED STATEMENT OF THE HON. JARED HUFFMAN, RANKING MEMBER, SUBCOMMITTEE ON WATER, POWER AND OCEANS

Mr. Chairman, this is the last week that we're here before heading back to our districts for 7 weeks. I want to point out that when we return, we only have 8 weeks left in this Congress. Yet instead of working on a number of important issues we've failed to address, we're here once again wasting taxpayer dollars on another farce of a hearing to attack the Endangered Species Act and blame environmental protections for California's drought, even though this preposterous claim has been debunked time and time again.

I guess I shouldn't be surprised. The leader of the Republican Party, Donald Trump, said recently, "There is no drought," and went on to make the same claims we'll hear today blaming water shortages on the Endangered Species Act. The Donald's statement on California's drought was rightfully mocked by experts and found to be false by non-partisan, independent fact checkers. Apparently my Republican colleagues ignored the memo on this, so let me share some facts now.

- Fact one, the 2014 water year was the third driest in recorded history and according to paleontological and tree-ring records, some experts conclude the current drought is California's most severe in 1,200 years. According to the U.S. Drought Monitor, 100 percent of California is currently experiencing some level of drought. To say there is no hydrological drought in California is simply absurd.
- Another fact, the Department of the Interior estimates that the Endangered Species Act accounted for a mere 2 percent of the water supply reduction in CVP water deliveries in 2014 and current estimates suggest a similarly small impact in 2015.
- Third, California's State Water Resources Control Board estimated that in 2015, of all the runoff in the Bay Delta watershed that flowed to San Francisco Bay—in other words the water that Donald Trump said was being "shoved out to sea"—only 2 percent of this water flowed out to the ocean solely for environmental protection. The vast majority of this water was released for salinity control to protect California's farm and drinking water supplies from being spoiled.

While we're in fact check mode, I also want to examine this notion that somehow California's farming industry is not getting water because of the Endangered Species Act. While some people with vested business interests have tried to peddle this fiction, the numbers tell a very different story. Even in this fifth year of historic drought, millions of acre-feet of water are being delivered to major agricultural water users. For example, one of the Republican witnesses before us today, the Tehama-Colusa Canal Authority, is expected to receive 100 percent of its maximum water allocation in 2016.

The other Republican witness represents another large group of agricultural water users—the Exchange Contractors—which is projected to receive 100 percent of its maximum water allocation of around 800 thousand acre-feet. Make no mistake, Mr. Chairman, a tremendous amount of water is being delivered to agriculture during this drought. In fact, if you average together total water deliveries this year for all CVP contractors, most of whom are agricultural water users, the CVP is projected to deliver approximately 60 percent of *maximum* contract quantities this year.

It's also true that much of this water has been made available because year after year state and Federal agencies have taken water that was supposed to be used to sustain California's fisheries and redirected it, primarily to powerful agricultural interests. Fisheries protections have been cut to the bone and the result has been a disaster for salmon fishermen.

Federal officials recently announced that there was a 97 percent mortality rate for juvenile Sacramento winter-run salmon in 2015. The year before, we had a 95 percent mortality rate. Fishery managers have severely restricted the commercial salmon season off the West Coast because of high salmon mortality in California. This comes after a failed salmon season last year and a virtually canceled Dungeness crab season.

Right now, many fishermen and their families are hanging on by a thread. Fishermen are struggling to pay mortgages. Boats are being sold or scrapped because their owners can't pay mooring fees. Homes have been repossessed. Restaurants, hotels and other retail and service businesses are struggling. Simply put, the human impact has been devastating on the many small business owners and workers whose livelihoods depend on healthy fish runs. Any further weakening of existing fishery protections will put many of California's fisheries and the jobs they support on the path to extinction.

While I agree that California's agricultural industry is important, it's long past time for the Republican Members of this subcommittee to recognize that there are thousands of other jobs in non-agricultural industries that also rely on California's water supply. Healthy ecosystems create and support jobs as well, and this subcommittee needs to recognize that the thousands whose jobs and livelihoods depend on water to maintain salmon and other fisheries matter in this debate.

I yield back.

———

Dr. FLEMING. The gentleman yields.
Dr. Gosar is now recognized.

STATEMENT OF THE HON. PAUL A. GOSAR, A REPRESENTATIVE IN CONGRESS FROM THE STATE OF ARIZONA

Dr. GOSAR. Thank you, Mr. Chairman, for holding this important hearing.

Today, we will hear another narrative of Federal dysfunction. Thanks to much needed precipitation this year, many Californians began to see the light at the end of the drought tunnel. Yet, here we are today holding another hearing on how two Federal fish agencies are making the light dimmer by undermining the water supply mission of another Federal agency, the Bureau of Reclamation.

Many in the western water world have been frustrated for years that the Bureau of Reclamation has not been able to stand up to the never-ending demands of the U.S. Fish and Wildlife Service, the National Marine Fisheries Service, and the litigants who fuel their missions. Based upon the testimony, today's circumstances are no different.

The fish agencies have based their latest demands on the premise that more water equals more fish. That notion has failed to work, as more water has been dedicated to fish, but their populations continue to dwindle, mainly due to ocean conditions, predatory fish, and other natural factors.

These agency proposals for more water midway through the irrigation season were not based on transparency. They not only failed to communicate adequately to water users, but they couldn't even communicate to each other. For example, one agency wanted to hold back water in reservoirs to supposedly benefit salmon, while the other wanted to drain the water to protect the Delta smelt.

These two agencies have direct jurisdiction over the Endangered Species Act, and it is clear they cannot harmonize their views on two different fish within the same watershed. It is time for a holistic approach on managing these species and to have one proposal, not two. Furthermore, these agencies need to be reorganized to avoid this situation. But don't take my word for it, take our President's, who proposed the same ideas a few years ago. So if you will look at the video, I would like to play 22 to 45.

[Video shown.]

Dr. GOSAR. He is referring to management of Pacific salmon and steelhead. Both agencies also manage Atlantic salmon and sea turtles, but as you will see today, both agencies manage species within the same watershed and there is simply no coordinated plan when these species' supposed needs conflict with each other. Meanwhile, the Bureau of Reclamation and its water users are left hanging in the political whims of this Administration.

For this reason, I am working with Mr. LaMalfa on this much needed reorganization proposal. This is just one way to fix this mess. There needs to be more transparency, more independent peer review, and more collaboration between Federal agencies themselves and with those who work with them.

What is clear is that the process is broken and that the Federal status quo is not working for species, farmers, ranchers, and communities that depend on our natural resources. Defending the way the agencies have done business in this latest California saga is similar to a doctor ignoring the causes of sickness that could be cured.

I look forward to today's hearing. And with that, I yield back.

[The prepared statement of Dr. Gosar follows:]

PREPARED STATEMENT OF THE HON. PAUL GOSAR, A REPRESENTATIVE IN CONGRESS FROM THE STATE OF ARIZONA

Thank you for holding this important hearing.

Today, we will hear another narrative of Federal dysfunction. Thanks to much-needed precipitation this year, many Californians began to see the light at the end of the drought tunnel. Yet, here we are today holding a hearing on how two Federal fish agencies are making that light dimmer by undermining the water supply mission of another Federal agency, the Bureau of Reclamation.

Many in the western water world have been frustrated for years that the Bureau of Reclamation has not been able to stand up to the never-ending demands of the U.S. Fish and Wildlife Service, the National Marine Fisheries Service, and the litigants who fuel their missions. Based upon the testimony, today's circumstance is no different.

The fish agencies have based their latest demands on the premise that more water equals more fish. That notion has failed to work, as more water has been dedicated to the fish, but their populations continue to dwindle mainly due to ocean conditions, predatory fish and other natural factors.

These agencies proposals for more water midway through the irrigation season were not based on transparency. They not only failed to communicate adequately to water users, but they couldn't even communicate to each other. For example, one agency wanted to hold back water in reservoirs to supposedly benefit salmon while the other wanted to drain the water to protect the Delta smelt.

These two agencies have direct jurisdiction over the Endangered Species Act and it's clear that they cannot harmonize their views on two different fish within the same watershed. It's time for a holistic approach on managing these species and to have one proposal, not two. Furthermore, these agencies need to be re-organized to avoid this situation. But, don't take my word for it, take our President's, who proposed the same idea a few years ago.

Watch video clip at https://www.youtube.com/watch?v=BFcWz9eyovA

Now, he's referring to management of Pacific salmon and steelhead. Both agencies also manage Atlantic salmon and sea turtles. But, as we will see today, both agencies manage species within the watershed and there's simply no coordinated plan when those species supposed needs conflict with each other. Meanwhile, the Bureau of Reclamation and its water users are left hanging in the political whims of this Administration.

For this reason, I'm working with Mr. LaMalfa on this much-needed reorganization proposal.

This is just one way to fix this mess. There needs to be more transparency, more independent peer review and more collaboration between Federal agencies themselves and with those who work with them.

What's clear is that the process is broken and the Federal status quo isn't working for species, farmers and ranchers and the communities that depend on our natural resources. Defending the way the agencies have done business in this latest California saga is similar to a doctor ignoring the causes of sickness that could be cured.

I look forward to today's hearing.

———

Dr. FLEMING. I thank the gentleman.

We are now ready to hear from our panel of witnesses. I will remind our panel that you will have 5 minutes to give your testimony, but whatever the length of your written testimony, it will be accepted as a permanent record.

First we have Mr. Jeffrey Sutton, General Manager of the Tehama-Colusa Canal Authority, from Willows, California.

Mr. David Murillo, Director of the Mid-Pacific Region of the Bureau of Reclamation in Sacramento, California. Mr. Murillo is accompanied by two individuals, Dr. Ren Lohoefener, Director of the Pacific Southwest Region of the U.S. Fish and Wildlife Service in Sacramento, and Mr. Barry Thom, Deputy Regional Administrator of the National Marine Fisheries Service in Portland, Oregon.

Then we have Mr. Bob Borck, a boat skipper based out of Eureka, California.

And finally, Mr. Ara Azhderian, Water Policy Administrator of the San Luis & Delta-Mendota Water Authority, which is based in Los Banos, California.

I now recognize Mr. LaMalfa to introduce the first witness.

STATEMENT OF THE HON. DOUG LaMALFA, A REPRESENTATIVE IN CONGRESS FROM THE STATE OF CALIFORNIA

Mr. LaMALFA. Thank you, Mr. Chairman. I appreciate you having this hearing and your attention to this tough issue we have going in California.

Over the last several decades, we have seen increasing regulatory requirements imposed on the Central Valley Project that have strangled its ability to provide water for all Californians. CVP is now operated with a stronger emphasis on managing flows for fish than for the millions of Californians who have built it and rely upon it.

Today, we are discussing two contradictory proposals by two wildlife agencies who, clearly, do not communicate with each other. One, NMFS, proposes drastically cutting water releases from the Shasta Reservoir to allegedly assist salmon, and cut Californians' water supply. The Fish and Wildlife Service proposes drastically increasing water releases from Shasta Reservoir, allegedly to assist Delta smelt, and cut Californians' water supplies.

I am really glad that Jeff Sutton could join us today. I have worked a long time with him in Northern California. He comes from the Tehama-Colusa Canal Authority. As their General Manager, he has worked tirelessly to find solutions on all sides of the issues, working collaboratively with the conservation interests as well as keeping the water flowing. So, Jeff, thank you for joining us today.

Mr. Chairman, thank you for the opportunity to introduce and comment.

Dr. FLEMING. OK. Mr. Sutton, you are now recognized for 5 minutes.

STATEMENT OF JEFFREY SUTTON, GENERAL MANAGER, TEHAMA-COLUSA CANAL AUTHORITY, WILLOWS, CALIFORNIA

Mr. SUTTON. Chairman Fleming, Ranking Member Huffman, and members of the subcommittee, thank you for this opportunity to speak today. Again, my name is Jeff Sutton. I am General Manager of the Tehama-Colusa Canal Authority.

I represent 17 water districts through 4 counties on the west side of the Sacramento Valley. We have a 140-mile canal system serving a variety of crops, about 1,000 family farms.

This California drought, everyone has suffered, communities have suffered, the environment has suffered, the fish have suffered, and the farmers have suffered. It has been a rough time. And let me tell you, this is an area that I am very passionate about. My family farming operation that I am involved in goes back to the 1870s. I am fifth generation and my son is number six, so we have been there a long time working for something we are proud of. A lot of our communities are a church, a Ford dealership, a John Deere dealership, and a fertilizer store. These are family farms that are proud of what they do, and finding ourselves kind of being defensive for the folks that provide the water that feeds our country and the Nation. It is just a strange place to be to see our farmers vilified in recent times. We believe we provide a lot to the country and the world.

The recent drought—2008 and 2009 were tough years. We had a couple good years between then, but 2014 and 2015 were extremely hard. For the Tehama-Colusa Canal Authority Service Area, we are those junior water right holders. We are CVP water service contracts, all 17 districts. We had zero percent allocation for 2 straight years. During that time, we fallowed upwards of 70,000 acres. We had to go through amazing gymnastics to prevent the destruction of permanent crops that could not be fallowed through some of those water transfers that, by the way, when we do those water transfers, we have to work with the U.S. Fish and Wildlife Service, because if the water cannot be delivered, a lot of land was put out because of the lack of ability to deliver. But if you want to transfer some from a senior water right holder, you have to jump through a lot of hoops and regulatory issues, CEQA, NEPA, to deal with the fact that you are going to fallow lands that have endangered giant garter snakes on them. And that is another species that is harmed by some of those actions that we are talking about today that are not even really analyzed in the scheme of this entire regulatory regimen. So, those are challenges that we have to work together to get through.

2015 came along—did it solve the problem? No. Congressman Huffman, is the drought completely over? No. But I will tell you, reading the *Sacramento Bee* flying in yesterday, Shasta Reservoir, that most of us rely on as the largest reservoir in California, is 108 percent of historical average today.

Finding ourselves at a time we rejoiced with 100 percent allocation, you are absolutely right, our district did get 100 percent allocation, and it actually set us up for what was a scarier year than 2014 and 2015 with these actions that have been proposed. We had National Marine Fisheries come in and want to reduce releases out of Shasta to the point that we could not even take water anymore. We would have been completely cut off, this after we had planted all our crops and made that investment, taken out loans, and taken our documents preparing for a bad year to do water transfers and threw them in the garbage can—they wouldn't have done us any good anyway, because it was too late to do water transfers. The lack of certainty after your planting date, after you have been awarded this, and the circumstances that would have befallen our farmers were an absolute tragedy.

Further—and I see my time is running terribly short—but we are also—independently of our own volition and cost, the NMFS action would have stopped us from doing something that we are spending our own money on to help Delta smelt, to run it through a bypass. We are pumping the water, we are operating and maintaining everything, and that would have been prohibited by what NMFS was doing.

In conclusion, we just have to find a way. The water users are engaged. Congressman Huffman, you know our Red Bluff project. I mean, we have done a lot. The fish have a better situation than ever, but we have to start working together. We need one biological opinion and we need collaboration and science-driven process while we work together to get one biological opinion, and help our farmers and the fish. Thank you.

[The prepared statement of Mr. Sutton follows:]

PREPARED STATEMENT OF JEFFREY P. SUTTON, GENERAL MANAGER, TEHAMA-COLUSA CANAL AUTHORITY

Chairman Fleming, Ranking Member Huffman, and members of the subcommittee, thank you for the opportunity to appear before you today.

INTRODUCTION

My name is Jeff Sutton, and I am the General Manager of the Tehama-Colusa Canal Authority (TCCA), a Joint Powers Authority comprised of seventeen (17) Water Districts, all of whom are Central Valley Project (CVP) Water Service Contractors.

The 150,000 acre service area that the TCCA serves spans four counties (Tehama, Glenn, Colusa, and Yolo Counties) along the west side of the Sacramento Valley, providing irrigation water to a diverse agricultural landscape and over 1,000 family farms that produce a variety of crops, including almonds, pistachios, walnuts, olives, grapes, prunes, rice, tomatoes, sunflowers, melons, vine seeds, alfalfa, and irrigated pasture. The water provided to these lands results in an annual regional economic benefit of over $1 billion.

The TCCA diverts water from the Sacramento River through the recently constructed Red Bluff Fish Passage Improvement Project, a quarter mile long, positive barrier, flat plate fish screen (one of the largest of its kind in the world), and new pumping plant, that provided for the retirement of the operation of the Red Bluff Diversion Dam, and the elimination of the fishery impacts associated therewith. This Project, implemented in partnership with the U.S. Bureau of Reclamation (USBR) created the capacity for reliable diversions of irrigation within the TCCA service area while also providing for unimpeded fish passage to prime spawning habitat on the upper Sacramento River for several threatened and endangered species (Winter and Spring Run Chinook Salmon, Steelhead, and Green Sturgeon). Included in the project is a 20+ acre mitigation site that includes extensive riparian habitat and a shallow side channel off the main stem of the Sacramento River designed specifically to benefit juvenile salmonid rearing habitat. The Red Bluff Fish Passage Project was recognized with the Association of California Water Agencies Clair Hill award for water project of the year, and the large water project of the year award from the district and western regional divisions of the American Society of Civil Engineers.

THE CALIFORNIA DROUGHT

From 2012–2015, California suffered greatly as a result of severe drought conditions. This prolonged dry period pushed the California water supply system to the breaking point at a time when it was already vulnerable due to a variety of factors including: continued population growth coupled with a lack of corresponding investment in new water infrastructure; and, most impactful, an increasingly burdensome regulatory environment that has continued to erode the supply side of the equation, reducing the flexibility, reliability, and operational viability of both the Central Valley Project and the State Water Project. As a result, severe and lasting impacts have been felt in all sectors during this drought crisis—urban, environmental, and agricultural.

In 2014 and 2015, for the first time in the history of the TCCA service area, all 17 water districts and 150,000 acres of prime farmland received an allocation of zero percent pursuant to their CVP water contracts. This resulted in extensive fallowing of farms (estimated at approximately 70,000 acres). In order to survive, TCCA growers resorted to the only alternative available to them. Paying others to fallow their fields, at great near-term expense in order to avoid the long-term economic catastrophe that would occur with the loss of permanent orchard crops.

These impacts have reverberated throughout our communities, and are not merely being felt by the farmers who have had to forego the planting of their fields. This crisis has also caused secondary impacts to agricultural based inputs (such as fuel companies, tractor companies, parts stores, fertilizer and seed companies, dryers, mills, and the local labor force), and tertiary impacts to other local businesses (stores, restaurants, auto dealers, etc.), as well as greatly affected local municipal services.

This historic lack of water supply has been felt throughout the CVP service area, with the Friant Water Authority and San Luis Delta Mendota Water Authority water districts also receiving a zero percent allocation in 2014 and 2015. That represents well over 2 million acres, of some of the most productive farmland in the world, receiving not a drop of surface water from the CVP. In these rural counties, these farms are the factories that fuel our economy. Without the water necessary to fuel this engine, it all comes to a screeching halt.

While the extremely dry period of hydrology currently being experienced in California has greatly contributed to the dire situation, regulatory actions, based on questionable science that have failed to provided the stated intentions of improving the fishery and environmental conditions, have frustrated efforts to effectively manage our water resources in an effective and efficient manner.

During similar California dry periods in 1977, and the drought experienced from the late 1980s through the early 1990s, while challenging, did not present the same desperation and impacts that are being felt today. During those experiences, reduced allocations occurred, but we were able to receive deliveries of 25–60 percent of the water to CVP agricultural water service contractors. Water storage projects were built to serve as our savings accounts during times of drought, a dynamic that had served us well. However reduced flexibility, lack of investment, and the repurposing of these resources for environmental purposes threaten the continued viability of our water supply system.

What has changed? First, legislative mandates and regulatory actions have resulted in lost water supply yield and reduced operational flexibility for our existing facilities. Second, permitting hurdles and a lack of coordination have prevented new projects from being realized.

Specifically, actions taken pursuant to the Central Valley Project Improvement Act, the USFWS and NMFS Endangered Species Act biological opinions related to the operations of the CVP, the Clean Water Act, and the Trinity Record of Decision have collectively impacted the deliveries of the CVP and the State Water Project (two of the largest water supply projects in the United States) by millions of acre-feet.

When combined, an absence of coordination coupled with regulatory hurdles have prevented any significant investment in new statewide water storage in California since the 1970s, during which time the population of the state has more than doubled. In short, while the demand for water has increased, our tools to manage and supply this vital resource have eroded. This is a recipe for disaster, and has resulted in impacts to California communities, agriculture, and the environment.

2016, A HOPE FOR RELIEF

During the winter of 2016 significant rains in Northern California relieved drought conditions at CVP and SWP facilities. For example, Shasta, Oroville, and Folsom reservoirs, all of which had been reduced to historic lows in the previous drought years, filled to over 100 percent of their historical capacity. The Sacramento, Yuba, and Feather River systems, as well as many of their tributaries, ran high throughout much of the winter and well into the spring, resulting in surplus conditions in the Bay Delta. Shasta's recovery, in particular, was a welcomed relief to the CVP, climbing from a low point of 1.3 million acre-feet (AF) (which was at 1.0 million AF in 2014) to peaking at over 4.2 million AF (with a capacity of 4.5 million AF). A significant improvement compared to the previous years, where the high water marks were 2.4 million AF and 2.7 million AF.

Further, the winter of 2016 provided a significantly increased and welcomed snow pack from previous years, as well as served to greatly benefit the regional aquifers that had been greatly exercised throughout the previous dry years. While the rumored "Godzilla El Niño" did not show up in full force, failing to provide complete recovery for all of California from the previous 4 dry years, it did significantly and substantially improve hydrologic conditions throughout the state, foretelling of an anticipated reprieve from the draconian water reductions and mandated conservation measures that befell California water agencies the previous 2 years.

On April 1 of 2016, the good news became official for TCCA water users and others, an allocation announcement from USBR of 100 percent for TCCA water users and other north of the Delta agricultural water service contractors, the Sacramento River Settlement Contractors, the San Joaquin Exchange Contractors, and for CVP M&I water users.

Friant water users did not see the same increases due to less recovery on the east side of the San Joaquin Valley, but did see significantly increased water allocations and it appeared would not have to fear a call on their water as a result of the inability to pump sufficient water to meet the contract terms for the Exchange Contractors, who have senior water rights on the San Joaquin River.

Due to regulatory conditions that greatly reduced USBR's ability to pump from the Delta throughout the winter and spring, despite the incredibly significant flows being experienced, the SLDMWA contractors continued to experience severe cutbacks, but did receive an allocation of 5 percent, with hope that circumstances could improve as the water year went on. This was a slight improvement over the previous 2 years that were zero percent. Unfortunately, hundreds of thousands of acre-feet of water were lost to the project as a result of the biological opinions that prevented water from being pumped and stored to provide some desperately needed relief to the farms and refuges on the west side of the San Joaquin Valley. This lost opportunity places further burden on the upstream reservoirs later in the year due to the inability to operate the CVP as planned. The Delta facilities allow for pumping to capitalize on the winter and spring flows below Shasta, and that accrue to the Delta, to be stored in San Luis Reservoir. This lost opportunity, due to regulatory constraints, continues to impair the ability to operate the CVP as designed, causing significant impacts throughout an integrated system.

FWS AND NMFS PROPOSALS

Shortly thereafter, the U.S. Fish and Wildlife Service (USFWS) and National Marine Fisheries Service (NMFS) proposed actions mandating mutually exclusive prescriptions that I believe posed a significant threat to the 2016 water operations plan of the CVP and its contractors.

The USFWS called for increased summer outflow that would require the release from upstream reservoirs of up to 300,000 AF of water for the stated purpose of improving smelt habitat. To my knowledge, summer outflow had never been considered as an action to benefit smelt and it is not a requirement pursuant to either of the last two intensive efforts to produce an ESA Biological Opinion for Delta smelt conducted by the USFWS. Further, the proposal failed to provide substantial scientific justification to merit what appeared to be little more than a high-risk gamble lacking an identifiable reward. The proposal also lacked adequate mechanisms to measure the outcomes of summer outflows giving rise to concerns that those proposing them might do so again in subsequent years regardless of the fact the potential benefits to the smelt could be non-existent while the negative impacts to those relying on the water being re-distributed would be certain. Additionally, the summer outflows were proposed well after the opportunity to acquire the needed quantities of water to achieve them had passed. There was no identification of funds to implement the action and it was implemented with complete disregard and lack of analysis to the impacts such an action would place on water users, refuges, other fish and wildlife and needs. Further, it ignored the impacts associated with repurposing this Federal funding that had been dedicated to other important environmental purposes.

Simultaneously, NMFS called for planned releases out of Shasta Reservoir to be reduced down to 8,000 cfs (significantly less than the temperature plan had called, up to 2,500 cfs less during peak demand periods in July) throughout the entire summer under claims that this was required to provide sufficient cold water throughout the season for endangered winter run Chinook salmon. NMFS claims mortality in 2014 and 2015 of 95 percent and 97 percent of winter run juveniles due to coldwater concerns. This claim is not wholly accurate due to their admitted lack of any monitoring during high flows on the upper Sacramento River at the Red Bluff facilities during high winter flows, the time these fish are most likely to migrate downstream. Further, NMFS proposed this ultra-conservative approach, despite assurances from USBR modeling that they could meet the requested temperature thresholds (that were greater than even called for in the NMFS BO).

As such, we had one agency calling for increased releases from upstream reservoirs for one species, while another called for severely reduced releases for another species. This, despite the fact that these actions are not included in any peer-reviewed regulatory requirement that has been through the prescribed Federal process or other analysis in regard to the potential impacts on the environment, the economy, or the health and welfare of the state of California.

THE IMPACTS

The impacts of the NMFS proposed action have already occurred to some degree, despite ultimately an agreement obtained by USBR's valiant efforts to ensure a more balanced interagency process. Throughout the months of May and June, reduced releases caused havoc on Sacramento River operations, resulting in some senior water contractors being shorted water supply, harm to irrigation pumping facilities due to low river elevations, water users having to alternatively pump groundwater wells at increased cost and from overly exercised aquifers due to the recent drought. Further, this has caused reduced ability to pump from the Delta to meet water allocations already announced south of the Delta, potentially resulting in shortages, after farmers had already taken out loans and expended significant funds to plant crops in reliance on receipt of water that was promised.

Had the prescribed operation that NMFS pursued been implemented, it would have led to an array of consequences, including the following:

1. TCCA water users and other north of the Delta water service contractors would likely have been substantially or completely deprived of the 100 percent allocation they were allocated, well after all their crops had been planted. This would have occurred after the time that they could have pursued water transfers, leaving them with little or no alternatives except to try to pump groundwater, where available, to enable their crops to survive. It is likely that most or all of the $1 billion of regional annual economic benefit that results from this farming activity would have been substantially lost. Most or all of the annual crops would have been destroyed, including the accompanying habitat benefits provided thereby, that provides significant waterfowl and wildlife habitat, including habitat for the endangered giant garter snake. Worse yet, tens of thousands of permanent crops would likely have been devastated as well. Permanent loss of these investments would have long lasting and deeply felt economic impact to the regional economy. Agricultural businesses and lending institutions would likewise be hard hit.

2. Settlement Contractors with senior water rights likewise would not have been able to divert all of the water that they are contractually entitled to, well after they had already planted and incurred substantial cost. This would have resulted in further significant losses in the Sacramento Valley as described above, and great loss of significant quantities of the primary habitat for a variety of specifies, including waterfowl and giant garter snake.

3. It is likely that this action would have led to the inability to meet the contractual obligation to the Exchange Contractors as well, resulting in them making a call on the water allocated to the Friant Water Users in Millerton Reservoir. This would cause significant impacts to both of these constituencies.

4. The actions to date still may, and certainly would have if fully implemented, deprived the contractors served by the SLDMWA of the slim 5 percent water allocation they received and planned for this year.

5. This action would have resulted in severe reductions to the refuge water supply to the detriment of the fish and wildlife, in particular the benefits to the waterfowl dependent on the Pacific Flyway.

6. The actions taken already have in increased pressure on Folsom Reservoir, requiring increased releases to make up for the reductions from Shasta. The proposed action, if fully implemented, likely would have placed the American River urban area in another year of panic, as bad, or worse than experienced the past 2 years.

In summary, the action proposed by NMFS would have had a domino effect throughout the entire CVP, resulting in severe impacts to communities, farms, and other fish and wildlife needs.

CONCLUSION

The CVP is suffering from a thousand cuts due to inconsistent and unbalanced regulatory requirements. Despite many of the reservoirs being filled in 2016, CVP operations are running on the ragged edge, failing to fulfill the needs of its contractors or the authorized purposes of the Project.

Despite billions of dollars of investment and millions of acre-feet being repurposed to benefit the fishery needs, as prescribed by the fishery agencies, we continue to see a continued decline in fish populations. CVPIA required 800,000 AF of water to be utilized for fishery purposes. The water users have funded the ecosystem restoration fund to provide billions in resources directed by these agencies to assist in fishery recovery. Every major upstream diversion has been fitted with a state-of-the-art fish screen. A temperature control device was added to Shasta Reservoir to benefit salmon. The biological opinions have continued to mandate further actions, reducing pumping and adding habitat restoration that have resulted in the rededication of more water to the environment and away from water users. Conditions for fish, according to the actions prescribed by the agencies, have never been better. Despite all of these efforts, the populations continue to decline. A more coordinated, science-driven and outcome-based approach is needed.

Single species management is not working, as evidenced by the current conflict between the above described smelt and salmon actions. For every action, there is a reaction. We need to pursue a coordinated, holistic, and more all encompassing approach to our problems in order to be successful. Working toward the development of a single NMFS and USFWS Biological Opinion for smelt and salmon would be a good place to start.

California water users are committed to working toward fishery solutions, but not at the expense of their livelihoods and this Nation's food supply. The Sacramento River Settlement Contractors have undertaken several actions in an effort improve fishery conditions, actions undertaken at their own volition and at their own expense. South of Delta SWP and CVP contractors have invested hundreds of millions of dollars trying to pursue viable solutions to identify workable solutions to the Delta problems. TCCA is currently partnering to assist on a project to increase food availability to Delta smelt, an action that the NMFS proposal would have prohibited. The Fish Passage Improvement Project at Red Bluff championed by the TCCA is further evidence of our commitment to solving problems.

A more robust process is needed to ensure that proposed regulatory actions are informed by sound science and directed at achieving measureable outcomes. In addition, greater priority should be given to ensure the interagency coordination needed to quantify how potential actions will impact all CVP water users and the environment.

If we do not find a way to work together in a more coordinated fashion that takes into account and respects all water needs, including the needs of our communities, agriculture and the environment, I fear we are headed for a future where both the Delta smelt and agriculture are extinct in California.

————

Dr. FLEMING. Thank you, Mr. Sutton.
Mr. Murillo, you are recognized.

STATEMENT OF DAVID MURILLO, MID-PACIFIC REGIONAL DIRECTOR, BUREAU OF RECLAMATION, U.S. DEPARTMENT OF THE INTERIOR

Mr. MURILLO. Chairman Fleming, Ranking Member Huffman, and members of the subcommittee, I am David Murillo, Regional Director of the Mid-Pacific Region of the Bureau of Reclamation. I am pleased to be here today to discuss changing demands on the Central Valley Project in California and actions we are taking to manage flow and temperatures for the benefit of fish, wildlife, and our water and power customers.

Joining me are Ren Lohoefener from the Fish and Wildlife Service, and Barry Thom from the National Marine Fisheries Services.

My written statement has been submitted for the record, so I will summarize that in the interest of time.

As of this month, the effects of an El Niño winter across California have left us with widely varying water supplies. Some facilities are near full, others are less than half capacity. As you know, despite the variability, Reclamation water users, like those beside me today, must operate facilities to balance competing demands and to comply with a suite of legal requirements.

In the case of the CVP, that means water rights permitting conditions from the California State Water Resource Control Board and biological opinions for the protection of fish listed under the State and Federal Endangered Species Act.

This spring and early summer, our agencies have been working on a temperature management plan for the Sacramento River, as required by the 2009 NMFS biological opinion and State Order 90–5, with the primary focus of protecting winter-run Sacramento River Chinook salmon. The plan is geared toward meeting obligations and maintaining commitments for operations of the CVP and State Water Project. The plan has also been developed to limit impacts to other beneficial uses, such as Folsom Reservoir levels, American River temperature, and Delta water quality.

The other option proposed, temperature management point, is at a location called Balls Ferry in Shasta County, keeping the river there at a 56-degree average daily temperature, as required under Order 90–5. Decisionmaking for significant changes in real-time operations is being coordinated among the partners, including Reclamation, NMFS, the Service, California Department of Water Resources, California Department of Fish and Wildlife, and the State Board.

As always, to the extent that Reclamation and the state can maximize export pumping from the Bay Delta, particularly during any sudden increases in Delta in-flow, we will continue to do so, just as we have done in the past. However, since the plan does fall somewhat short of the planned schedule for releases to the Sacramento River this summer, some adjustments to the 2016 CVP allocations are possible. Throughout this process, we work closely and transparently with CVP water users to explore this possibility. We will continue that collaboration.

That said, and with progressively dryer conditions this summer, we are encouraging communities to continue to conserve water and operate as efficiently as possible. We recognize that has become business as usual for most water users, some of whom are alongside me here today. While I cannot give any guarantees as to how the year will play out, Reclamation stands ready to adjust operations to improve temperature conditions if needed. Equally, Reclamation expects the real-time monitoring and adjustment opportunities provided for in the plan to allow essential flexibility to enable to us meet our commitments, while operating within what will be close confines of the law. I hope that the many jointly funded projects our agencies pursue each year with the water users and environmental communities are evidence of our strong ongoing partnership. At the operational, financial, and policy levels, we are committed to helping California succeed in all years, not just in times of drought, flood, or environmental crises.

In closing, we would like to thank the subcommittee for its attention to this issue. These past several years have been incredibly challenging, and we are proud of the collaboration and creativity the stakeholders have shown in finding ways to manage this complicated and important system.

This concludes my statement. I would be pleased to answer any questions at the appropriate time. Thank you.

[The prepared statement of Mr. Murillo follows:]

PREPARED STATEMENT OF DAVID MURILLO, REGIONAL DIRECTOR, MID-PACIFIC REGION, BUREAU OF RECLAMATION, U.S. DEPARTMENT OF THE INTERIOR

Chairman Fleming, Ranking Member Huffman and members of the subcommittee, I am David Murillo, Regional Director for the Mid-Pacific Region of the Bureau of Reclamation (Reclamation). I am pleased to represent the Department of the Interior (Department) today to discuss changing demands on the Central Valley Project (CVP) in California, and actions we are taking with our partner agencies to manage river flow and temperatures in 2016 for the benefit of fish, wildlife, and our water and power customers.

In February of this year, Reclamation presented testimony before this subcommittee describing how 4 years of brutal drought in California were transitioning into an El Niño water year in 2015–2016. We discussed how these 4 drought years have severely reduced snowpack, drawn down reservoir levels and brought about significant groundwater withdrawals that have taken their toll on California's water users, the environment, the economy and communities across the state. We cautioned against the misguided hope of many that one El Niño year would be enough to correct for the long running, persistent drought. Against that backdrop, we referenced what I continue to see as innovative local agreements, adaptive management, and resilience that have all been essential to the survival of many farms and small communities.

Today I can provide an update on conditions, and on the temperature and flow considerations that have occupied a great deal of the time, energy, and concern for me and the other witnesses here today.

As of this month, the effects of an El Niño winter across California have left the state with widely varying water supplies in its network of local, state, and Federal reservoirs. Precipitation above the CVP's Shasta Lake was abundant enough this past winter that Shasta Dam spent several weeks during the spring in or near flood control operations. Conditions in the Trinity River Division of the CVP were also improved over recent years. Trinity Reservoir is currently at 70 percent of the 15-year average as of today, and significant releases have been made to the Trinity River to support the Trinity River Restoration Program consistent with the Program's 2000 Record of Decision. Further to the south, while Folsom Lake on the American River reached elevations requiring flood control releases during the winter, drought conditions on that basin can still be felt. Unfortunately, conditions on the San Joaquin River Basin were much dryer, such that New Melones Reservoir is at only 44 percent of its 15-year average for this date. These storage levels illustrate the challenging results of 1 year of average to below-average hydrology when combined with long-standing drought in these important basins.

Even in the face of these varying hydrologic conditions, Reclamation must operate the CVP to balance the competing demands and to comply with a suite of legal requirements, including water rights permitting conditions by the California State Water Resources Control Board (State Board) and biological opinions (BiOps) for the protection of fish species listed under the state and Federal Endangered Species Acts (ESA). The National Marine Fisheries Service's (NMFS) 2009 BiOp covers ESA-listed steelhead, Chinook salmon and sturgeon, and the U.S. Fish and Wildlife Service's (Service) 2008 BiOp applies to Delta smelt. Temperature considerations are required under the 2009 NMFS BiOp as well as State Board Order 90–5 for the benefit of species in the Sacramento River and conditions in the Bay Delta. This spring and early summer our agencies have been working on a 2016 temperature management plan for the Sacramento River as required by the 2009 NMFS BiOp and Order 90–5, with the primary focus of protecting critically endangered Sacramento River winter-run Chinook salmon. I know the 2016 Sacramento River Temperature Management Plan (SRTMP) is one of the central topics of the subcommittee's interest today, and I will focus the remainder of my statement on this matter.

In late June and early July, Reclamation, NMFS and the state of California finalized plans to operate the CVP and Shasta Dam consistent with temperature requirements for winter-run Chinook salmon and transmitted the plan to the State Board. We believe the plan avoids excessive mortality to winter-run Chinook salmon that would violate the ESA while allowing some flexibility to operate the CVP and State Water Project (SWP) to allow Reclamation to take other actions, recommended by scientists at the Service, to augment Delta outflow for the benefit of critically imperiled Delta smelt, also listed under the ESA. The SRTMP recommends an approach to maintain a 56.0° F daily average temperature through the end of September, while ensuring that the limited supply of cold water behind Shasta Dam can be fully and strategically utilized throughout the season. In addition, this approach helps Reclamation meet other obligations and maintain commitments for operation of the CVP and SWP. The SRTMP has also been developed to limit impacts to other beneficial uses, such as Folsom Reservoir levels, American River temperature management for species protection, and Delta water quality. The over-arching proposed temperature compliance point is a location called Balls Ferry in Shasta County, and Order 90–5 requires, keeping daily average water temperature in the River at this location at 56.0° F. The SRTMP calls for actual daily releases to be based on real-time monitoring to ensure that temperature compliance is accomplished, and other downstream diversion, flow, and Delta requirements are met. Decision-making for significant changes in real-time operations is being further coordinated among the partners including Reclamation, NMFS, the Service, California Department of Water Resources (DWR), California Department of Fish and Wildlife, and the State Board (collectively, the state and Federal agencies).

The SRTMP includes monitoring activities throughout the summer and fall, and check-in points to ensure that sufficient cold water reserves are being maintained to meet the temperature management objectives identified in the plan. In the event that monitoring shows that cold water reserves are being depleted in a way not envisioned in the plan (*i.e.*, if the volume of Shasta Reservoir water <49° F is less than 95 percent of the volume forecast in the plan), action will be required to ensure that the temperature objectives can be met, even if those actions have water supply implications. As always, to the extent that Reclamation and the state can opportunistically maximize export pumping from the San Francisco Bay-Delta (Delta), particularly during any sudden increases in Delta inflow, we will continue to do so just as we have done in the past. However, since the SRTMP does fall somewhat short of the previously announced schedule for releases to the Sacramento River this summer, some adjustment to 2016 CVP allocations is possible. In the coming weeks, we will be working diligently with all CVP water user groups to explore options and tools to address this possibility in a reasonably equitable manner. That said, and with progressively drier hydrologic conditions throughout the Central Valley this summer, our agencies are encouraging communities to continue to conserve water and operate as efficiently as possible. We recognize that philosophy has become business-as-usual for many water users, some of whom are alongside me here today.

The success of the SRTMP is predicated on how closely actual operations align with the predicted hydrologic modeling results. Therefore, the SRTMP includes multiple commitments for frequent updates to detailed temperature profiles, modeling projections, temperature control device gate operations, and meteorological data via weekly and monthly conference calls, meetings, and data exchanges. While I cannot give any guarantees as to how the year will play out, Reclamation stands ready to adjust operations to improve temperature conditions and continue compliance with the SRTMP if needed as the season progresses. Equally, Reclamation expects that the real-time monitoring and adjustment opportunities provided for in the plan will allow it the flexibility that is essential to help enable us to meet our commitments while operating within the law.

The development of the SRTMP is itself another example of the ongoing collaborative work being undertaken by a broad array of parties involved in California water management issues. Since December 2013, state and Federal agencies that supply water, regulate water quality, and protect California's fish and wildlife have worked closely together to manage through the drought and problem-solve with the larger stakeholder community. The state and Federal agencies have coordinated CVP and SWP operations at the highest level possible, to manage water resources through both forward-thinking and real-time efforts. This cooperative environment has allowed our agencies, working with the State Board, to take advantage of modifications to operational standards required under Orders 90–5 and 1641 (D–1641). Those collaborative actions have borne fruit, and without the Temporary Urgency Change Petitions approved by the State Board, collective CVP and SWP reservoir storage would have been 880,000 acre-feet lower last summer, further depleting cold water pool and creating dangerously low storage levels.

Finally, while we understand that today's hearing is focused on the operational issues playing out this summer, I want to reiterate what we have said before about the Department's commitment to working with the state of California on the long-term goals of improving California's water supply reliability, and protecting and restoring the Bay-Delta environment. I hope that the many jointly funded projects our agencies pursue each year with the water user and environmental communities in

California are evidence of that ongoing partnership. At the operational, financial, and policy levels, we are committed to helping California succeed in all years, not just in times of drought, flood or environmental crisis.

The Obama administration remains committed to collaborating with the state of California and other stakeholders throughout California through the National Drought Resilience Partnership (NDRP) that President Obama recently established. As our climate changes, resilience to long-term drought, especially in California, is a critical issue every level of government needs to put as a priority. We look forward to working together with California on this as well.

In closing, we would like to thank the subcommittee for its attention to this issue. These past several years have been incredibly challenging and we are proud of the collaboration and creativity that all the stakeholders have shown in finding ways to manage this complicated and important system.

That concludes my statement. I would be pleased to answer questions at the appropriate time.

———

Dr. FLEMING. Thank you, Mr. Murillo.

I now recognize the Ranking Member for an introduction.

Mr. HUFFMAN. Thanks, Mr. Chairman.

It is an honor for me to welcome and to introduce Bob Borck, who is a commercial fisherman in Eureka, California. Right now, our commercial fishermen, their families, and the communities that they are a part of are hanging by a thread. They have had a failed salmon season last year. We had an unprecedented mostly closure of the very important Dungeness crab fishery because of an algae bloom, and some boats are being sold and marinas are struggling.

Mr. Borck is here to remind us that on the fisheries side of this equation there are also real people, real communities, Ford dealerships, churches, boat dealers, and Rotary clubs. There is a human element to that side of this system as well, and I welcome Mr. Borck here to tell us a bit about it.

STATEMENT OF BOB BORCK, SKIPPER, FISHING VESSEL BELLE J II

Mr. BORCK. Good morning, members of the committee. Thank you so much for allowing me to be here today. My name is Bob Borck. I am owner-operator of a fishing vessel called the Belle J II, moored in Eureka, California.

Eureka happens to be basically the middle of salmon coast from Washington down into Santa Cruz. We are dead set in the middle of it, and we are a port that may never ever have another regular salmon season again, for other reasons than Central Valley water, but, again, we are a port that will never fish out of our own town again for a full season.

The U.S. salmon troll fleet is in trouble. There is no other way to put it. You have the Sacramento-San Joaquin fish. They are the bulk of what we fish on here in California. They are also a huge component of what gets caught in Oregon. They are caught off Washington. There have been net pen fish that were raised at, I believe it was Half Moon Bay, that were put in the ocean to increase our ability to catch. They are caught as far north as Alaska. You look at the Columbia River, they are the mainstay of Washington and Alaska troll salmon.

The problem is freshwater in inland watersheds. If you don't have enough freshwater for spawners to go up and you don't have enough freshwater for smolts to survive to get out, you lose your fishery. That is what we have had with the drought.

Assuming that this drought ends and we get all happy and there is lots of water again, it will be 3 years before the troll fleet sees a successful season. You have to have plenty of water to flush the smolts out of the river system and avoid predation. It takes water.

On the coast, you have at least 30,000 jobs, well over a billion dollars in economic benefit that happens. You have 2,000 commercial permit holders up and down the coast in the different states. Most of those boats have crews. There are all the support businesses on land, from Englund Marine, where I buy rope and buoys and all the parts and pieces that it takes to keep the boat going, to when I am stuck in Coos Bay and the wind is blowing, I am eating in restaurants and staying in hotels. Water is the issue.

Last year, I ended up spending the end of July and most of August in Oregon. I had four trips in a row with one or two fish per trip. I did not cover the expenses of the ice, let alone the cost of the fuel, let alone being away from home for 6 straight weeks. This year, Jeff French, fishing out of Half Moon Bay, had five fish in four trips. He too did not make his expenses. The Alaska troll king fishery that started July 1 lasted a grand total of 5 days. Their allocation was mopped up in 5 days.

Heather Sears, who has a boat out of Southern California, she leased a Washington permit. I think she told me she spent $8,000 leasing the permit. She figures she is not even going to put a hook in the water in Washington because their allocation for fish was so small, it wasn't even worth trying. She drove right past there and went to Alaska and had her 5 days.

There is an incredible cost to doing business here. I have lost $150,000 in the last 7 years trying to buy in and get a commercial fishing operation off the ground. Part of it is bad timing because of the drought, because we don't have water, because we don't have adequate salmon seasons.

People are hurting. Trucks are being repossessed. People are losing homes. Why? Because we don't have an adequate way to go take our boats and do what used to be done 30, 40, 50 years ago with ease. And a lot of it has to do with the fact that we don't have enough salmon, and we don't have enough salmon because we don't have enough water.

Thank you very much.

[The prepared statement of Mr. Borck follows:]

PREPARED STATEMENT OF BOB BORCK, EUREKA, CALIFORNIA COMMERCIAL SALMON, CRAB AND BLACK COD FISHERMAN

Good morning Mr. Chairman and members of the committee. I'm Bob Borck, skipper of the fishing vessel Belle J II. I fish salmon, crab and black cod commercially out of Eureka in Northern California. I've come here today so you can hear from the coast.

Our salmon fishery is in trouble and let me start by reminding you all that salmon spend part of their lives in California's rivers and streams, where they're born and die, and part of their lives in the ocean. I'm here to report to you that the ocean is doing its part for salmon. The problems confronting California salmon are all caused by man-made changes to California's rivers, streams, and Bay Delta. Biggest among these is lack of river flows to the sea in the spring which are needed to deliver baby salmon to the ocean.

We rely on Central Valley fall run king salmon which are fished from Santa Barbara to Washington. These fish come from the Sacramento River, the source of much of the water at issue today. We are blessed to have these fish and so are our consumers, who snap them up as soon as we bring them to port.

These fish are the cornerstone of 23,000 jobs in California and 11,000 in Oregon in a "normal" non-drought year. The industry serving both sport and commercial salmon generates about $1.4 billion in economic activity by the time you add in all the multipliers and about half that much again in jobs and dollars in Oregon where as much as 60 percent of their ocean caught salmon originate in California's Central Valley.[1]

But we haven't had a really good salmon season since 2013. I think it's informative to consider what gave us a good season in that year since it highlights what's hurting us now. The good 2013 season was fueled by two things:

1. strong new salmon protections coming out of the Endangered Species Act's 2009 salmon biological opinion, and
2. a wet winter and spring in 2010/11.

The 2009 ESA protections gave us a break from the crushing diversion of salmon water from the Bay Delta we experienced prior to 2009. It finally gave baby salmon a little water to make it to the ocean. Spring runoff from the Central Valley functions like a conveyor belt that carries baby salmon downstream from where they were born and out to the ocean. They are poor swimmers and need strong spring river flows to the ocean to survive. When this water is diverted in the Delta, the conveyor belt carrying these baby salmon is cut and they die.

The massive volumes of water diverted from the Bay Delta prior to 2009 coincided with the first ever total shut down of ocean salmon fishing in California in 2008 and 2009.[2] Salmon born in years that saw all time high water diversions from the Bay Delta basically failed to survive and return as adults 2 years later.

The 2008 and 2009 shutdown was a desperate time for the salmon industry. We had to resort to Federal disaster relief to get through the closure, which is no way to run a business. We're not looking for a handout. We want a fishery.

This year, we're staring down some of the slimmest fishing opportunity since the 2008–09 closure because of low salmon production in California's rivers, caused by drought and water diversions.

Low forecasts salmon abundance and problems with the Bureau of Reclamation's management of cold water at Shasta dam for the last 2 years forced the Pacific Fishery Management Council to severely restrict our time on the ocean this year. In the southern half of California, those fleets only got 2 months to fish in what used to be the April–October salmon season. Right now we're shut down, statewide, for the entire month of July, which is usually one of our most productive times to fish.

Today, as I sit here, I and all virtually all California and Oregon salmon/crab fishermen are reeling from brutal back to back to back fishing seasons. 2015's salmon harvest was significantly lower than projected. We had to delay the 2015–16 Dungeness crab season for concerns over domoic acid. The delay cost us our best markets and weather windows to fish.

When fishing was on, it was poor, as expected. Jeff French, a fisherman in Morro Bay, California, landed only five salmon over four fishing trips during the 2-month span this year. His salmon season is over. He'll be forced to fall back on rock crab, a much less lucrative fishery, until the Dungeness crab season starts back up in September.

And it's not just the southern part that's suffered poor fishing this year. Sarah Bates, a San Francisco fisherwoman recently returned from a 3-day trip with only eight salmon. This is not normal, and not for lack of effort.

Baby salmon, at a year of age, make it to sea in large numbers riding that heavy rain runoff. In addition to giving them a ride, the runoff also gives them camouflage in muddy water turbidity. This effectively "cloaks" the baby salmon, making them invisible to predatory fish that would eat them. I know many of you believe predator fish are the main cause of salmon decline but I'm here to tell you it's the lack of camouflage in the form of muddy runoff that makes baby salmon vulnerable to predators in the rivers and Delta.

So contrary to what we've seen reported from some that know nothing about salmon or the ecological function of the Bay Delta, water flowing to the sea is not wasted! The most obvious evidence of this is the good fishing seasons we always get

---

[1] http://asafishing.org/newsroom/news-releases/economic-data-supports-efforts-to-recover-californias-salmon-fisheries/.

[2] http://www.dailydemocrat.com/general-news/20090119/weak-oversight-brought-us-to-depleted-delta.

2 years after heavy rains. The heavy rain runoff mimics pre-dam natural runoff patterns that salmon evolved to thrive in.

There's a good example of the value of spring flows to salmon in the Columbia River basin. After years of court battles, like those we have here in California, a Federal judge in 2005 ordered reservoir managers up there to release water to flush baby salmon in the spring.

The results have been dramatic, with probably the greatest recovery of West Coast salmon in history. The last few years have seen modern record returns of salmon to the Columbia River which has provided a great economic boost to that region.

I'd like to speak a little more on the make up of the salmon industry. Most of us fishermen make a living family wage in good years. We're not getting rich, but we can save a little and get ahead after really wet years when we always get a bump in salmon numbers. Lately, we've been getting poor and spending the last of our savings, in large part, due to depressed salmon numbers caused by lack of fresh-water for those fish in the Central Valley.

People flock to the coast to catch a salmon when fishing is good. They come from hundreds of miles and bring their wallets with them. Word of a hot salmon bite is akin to word of a gold strike 150 years ago. It gets people moving in the direction of the salmon.

Our boats benefit from new equipment and updated maintenance after a good season. The opposite is also true. Maintenance is deferred and we're stuck with patched up gear after poor seasons and as you can imagine, this can lead to less than safe working conditions for us.

Businesses that rely on both sport and commercial salmon include places like Englund Marine, a chain of stores supplying fishing and boating needs in California and Oregon. We've got one in Eureka and it does well when salmon are doing well.

The salmon industry also fuels many West Coast machine shops, boat yards and boat dealerships, tackle and gear stores, seafood buyers, local hotels and restaurants, and ports and harbors. They all benefit when salmon fishermen are in town and they all suffer when salmon numbers are low.

But we're already seeing a decline in our salmon industry, as critical fishing infrastructure like fuel and ice docks have begun to disappear from harbors in quintessential ports like Monterey and Santa Cruz.

This industry is vitally important to rural California where most of our harbors exist. It's vital to the many thousands of families that rely on salmon for their livelihoods. It's vital to the cultural fabric of our coastal communities.

I want to leave you with the understanding that Federal protections for salmon under the Endangered Species Act are the only reason we in California are still on the water fishing. They are the only reason we still have any salmon in California rivers. Without ESA salmon protections we lose all of our Central Valley wild salmon runs, and in all likelihood, the salmon industry. It's important to understand that although ESA salmon protections are geared to two of the four king salmon runs in the Central Valley, the other two, which we rely on, also greatly benefit from these ESA protections. This is why the West Coast salmon fleet supports the ESA.

State and Federal fish agencies tell us we lost between 95 and 98 percent of our Central Valley salmon during the last 2 drought years. The eggs didn't hatch because river water released from reservoirs was too warm. We don't manage the reservoirs, and we didn't cause that wipe out. But we're doing our part by limiting the number of fish we catch, to make sure that we have a fishery into the future. I ask that you do your part to make sure that California's water resources are allocated in a way that's equitable and protective of all of California's industries.

We've got fishing families in Crescent City, Eureka, Fort Bragg, Bodega Bay, San Francisco Bay, throughout Monterey Bay and beyond whose futures are hanging in the balance. They've been practicing a sustainable lifestyle in harmony with our natural systems for decades and providing one of the most incredible foods known to man.

We've got an incredible ocean off the most beautiful coast in the Nation that's short on a key resource needed not only by us humans, but also many other species that need salmon. I appeal to each of you to act for the long-term benefit of the great state we call home and that means leaving enough water in our salmon rivers for salmon to survive. Thank you.

———

Dr. FLEMING. Thank you.

The Chair now recognizes Mr. Azhderian for 5 minutes.

STATEMENT OF ARA AZHDERIAN, WATER POLICY ADMINIS-
TRATOR, SAN LUIS & DELTA-MENDOTA WATER AUTHORITY

Mr. AZHDERIAN. Good morning, Mr. Chair, Ranking Member Huffman, and members of the committee. It is an honor to be here with you today.

If there is one thing that I would ask you to remember about today, it is that California is at yet another crossroads in how we manage endangered species and water supply. The decisions that will be made in the coming weeks and months will have impacts probably for years.

The testimony you have heard from the Federal agencies and will hear from the Federal agencies is really aimed at assuaging the concerns about how we are managing both fish and water. What I found interesting in the testimony is not what they say so much, but rather what they don't say.

There is nothing about how other stressors are being dealt with, there is nothing about the ill-conceived summer flow proposal that is more likely to hurt Delta smelt than to help them, and is in clear conflict with temperature management objectives for winter-run salmon. There is nothing about what happens to the millions of Californians that are dependent on the CVP water supply if things do not go as planned. There is nothing about the water supply impacts that are already beginning to accrue into 2017; rather, it is an expression of a false confidence about a status quo, insular, single-species, single-stressor approach that somehow will work this time.

For a quarter of a century now, National Marine Fisheries Service and the Fish and Wildlife Service have been responsible for the protection and recovery of winter-run salmon and Delta smelt. The status of winter-run salmon is poor, not the worst we have seen, but poor. Delta smelt numbers, of course, are at historic lows. And throughout this time at each crossroads, the decision has been to continue to manage our fisheries in the same manner, this despite broad recognition from the onset that comprehensive solutions and collaboration was the way to proceed.

In the early 1990s, the environmental community, water users, and the state and Federal Government all recognized the need for collaboration and comprehensive solutions, and agreed when they signed the Bay Delta accord, to move forward in that fashion. Unfortunately, that did not occur. In the decades following, numerous independent science panels have warned us of sticking to this approach, of not researching the biological causal effects of these fisheries' declines. In 2009, the state of California reaffirmed the need for comprehensive solutions when it passed the Delta Reform Act. This is not new advice. It has just been ignored.

So we have a choice. It is critical to remember we have a choice. This crossroad provides an opportunity to broaden participation in the process, to reassess our current failed approaches, to research causal effects, enlist stakeholder support, demand accountability about the results, and refine and redirect our actions or reject them based upon demonstrable benefits and evidence.

In the end, changing demands is not about Ag. and municipal use. We are among the most efficient users of water in the world. It is about unbridled regulation. And water supply uncertainty is about the unceasing demand for more water for environmental use without accountability. After a quarter century, and fish populations, water supplies, and the people who care about both worse off than ever, it is time that we deserve better environmental protection.

I thank you for the opportunity to speak here today and look forward to any questions you may have. Thank you.

[The prepared statement of Mr. Azhderian follows:]

PREPARED STATEMENT OF ARA AZHDERIAN, WATER POLICY ADMINISTRATOR, SAN LUIS & DELTA-MENDOTA WATER AUTHORITY

INTRODUCTION

Mr. Chairman, Ranking Member Huffman and members of the subcommittee, my name is Ara Azhderian, Water Policy Administrator for the San Luis & Delta-Mendota Water Authority (Authority). Thank you for the opportunity to appear before you today to testify on the causes of uncertainty affecting the water supply of the eighth largest economy in the world, the state of California.

The San Luis & Delta-Mendota Water Authority (Authority) is a Joint Powers Authority under California law that was formed in 1992. The Authority serves 29 member agencies, 27 of which hold contracts for water with the U.S. Department of the Interior Bureau of Reclamation's (Reclamation) Central Valley Project (CVP). Our members manage water to serve agricultural, municipal, and environmental purposes. Our service area is approximately 3,300 square miles and spans all or parts of 8 counties: Contra Costa, Santa Clara, San Joaquin, Stanislaus, Merced, San Benito, Fresno, and Kings. Roughly, our northern border is the southern edge of the Sacramento-San Joaquin Rivers Delta (Delta), our eastern border is the San Joaquin River, our southern border is California State Highway 41, and our western border is the Santa Cruz Mountains. Our members provide water to 5 of the Nation's top 10 agricultural producing counties, to the second largest contiguous wetlands in the United States after the Florida Everglades, and to approximately 2 million Californians living in communities ranging from small, rural, often disadvantaged towns like Avenal and Huron, to the affluent global center of technology, Silicon Valley. If you have eaten a cantaloupe, used a can of tomato sauce or jar of salsa, "googled" on an iPhone, or just appreciate the majesty of birds migrating the Pacific Flyway, the chances are good that you've been touched by CVP water.

BACKGROUND

Since formation of the Authority, drought has been the center of our universe. In 1992, California was in the fifth year of a natural drought, a hydrologic situation not dissimilar from today. In the worst of it, CVP agricultural water service (Ag Service) contractors were allocated 25 percent of their contract supply. Concurrently with the natural drought, regulatory changes were happening in rapid succession, first with the listings of winter-run salmon and Delta smelt under the Federal Endangered Species Act, the reprioritization of CVP water supplies under the Central Valley Project Improvement Act, and new water quality standards under California's delegated Clean Water Act authority. The water supply reductions resultant of the natural drought made it difficult to comprehend what the water supply impacts of the regulatory drought would be once the rains returned. As the dust settled over the next few years, it became clear that the regulatory drought had reduced the CVP water supply for south of Delta Ag Service contractors by about 35 percent on average. Many small farms vanished, many acres were constantly fallowed, many jobs were lost, and several once vibrant agricultural communities became shells of their former selves.

In response, farmers did what they do best, adapt. The new regulatory water supply gap would be expensive to close, so farmers started planting higher value crops. With the increased revenue, they began investing in state-of-the-art irrigation systems, reusing and recycling drain water, and purchasing water for transfer, a big portion of which came from Northern California. By the late 1990s, as some stability returned, efforts turned toward restoring the water supply lost to the regulatory drought. The center of this effort was known as CALFED, an enterprise aimed at improving both the environment and water supply. However, despite billions of dollars spent and millions of acre-feet dedicated to the cause, by the mid 2000s new, startling fish abundance declines were underway, affecting Delta smelt and winter-run salmon, among others. With respect to Delta smelt, the Interagency Ecological Program Pelagic Organism Decline Progress Report: 2007 Synthesis of Results identified numerous possible causes for the decline, including contaminants, predation, and lack of food, and stated, "Entrainment at the CVP and SWP pumps also seems to be an unlikely single cause of POD but may be important in some years for some species." Regarding salmon, both the National Marine Fisheries Service (NMFS) and Pacific Fishery Management Council concluded that the sudden decline was caused by poor ocean conditions. PFMC stated in their March 2009 report "What caused the Sacramento River fall Chinook stock collapse?" that "The evidence pointed to ocean conditions as the proximate cause because conditions in freshwater were not unusual, and a measure of abundance at the entrance to the [Bay-Delta] estuary showed that, up until that point, these broods were at or near normal levels of abundance." Yet, despite numerous scientific reports identifying multiple causes driving the new fish declines, the U.S. Fish and Wildlife Service (FWS) and National Marine Fisheries Service (NMFS) chose to do what they have always done, implement single stressor, single species regulations, primarily on the CVP and California State Water Project (SWP) (collectively Projects), while doing little to address the myriad of other known stressors.

In 2008 and 2009, the FWS and NMFS issued new biological opinions (BiOp), the primary focus of which is to curtail pumping. While the BiOps do call for other actions, like habitat restoration, no action has been as vigorously implemented as the pumping constraints. Like the regulations implemented in the early 1990s, these too were implemented during a natural drought period so the "real world" water supply costs have been difficult to determine. Water operations modeling suggests that the BiOps have cut CVP and SWP water supplies by about another 30 percentage points. For south of Delta Ag Service contractors, this translates to a long-term average water supply of about 35 percent of contract. The current BiOps have squeezed virtually all of the operational flexibility from the Projects, causing the damaging effects of the natural drought to amplify the chronic water supply shortages of the regulatory drought, with devastating effect throughout the CVP service area, but especially in the San Joaquin Valley. Over the last 4 years, CVP south of Delta Ag Service water supply allocations have been 20 percent, 0 percent, 0 percent, and 5 percent. In 2014, for the first time in the history of the CVP, Reclamation had to draw CVP water from the east side of the San Joaquin Valley for delivery to the west side, and to borrow water from individual farmers and districts, because it could not meet its contractual and statutory obligations to provide water to prior water rights holders and managed wetlands from traditional sources of supply in the north. In addition, over 2 million acres of farmland received no CVP water whatsoever and CVP supplies to municipalities were approximately 30 percent of historical average, significantly lower than the minimum called for in Reclamation's Municipal & Industrial Shortage Policy. These disasters were repeated in 2015.

Since imposition of the BiOps, Federal agencies have steadfastly claimed that the unprecedented water supply shortages that have followed have been the result of the natural drought, not a regulatory drought. As recently as February 24 before this very subcommittee, Reclamation's Mid-Pacific Region's Director David Murillo reiterated, "While some have argued the state's water supply cutbacks are entirely due to environmental regulations, *it has been drought—the extreme declines in annual precipitation and snowpack in California since 2012—far more than any other factor* [emphasis added], that has constrained the ability of the state and Federal projects to deliver full allocations of water during these years." Clearly natural drought plays a role in water supply, this has always been the case and is a major reason why the Projects were built, but a review of the volume of water stored in Shasta Reservoir [Attachment 1] clearly demonstrates that it is how the water is used that affects water supply allocations, much more than how much there is of it. The red line represents 1977, the benchmark dry year, the blue line represents 1991, the fourth year of that 5-year drought cycle, the green line represents 2015, the fourth year of our most recent drought cycle, and the heavy blue line represents this year. The corresponding CVP south of Delta Ag Service water supply allocations for these 4 example years are 25 percent, 25 percent, 0 percent, and 5 percent. And it is not just the volume of water in storage that has been affected, but too our ability to capture water at critical times. Attachment 2 illustrates all of the missed opportunities this year to pump water when it was abundant in the Delta. The color coded background indicates what regulation was generally causing the restriction over some period of time. The dashed, variable line indicates the volume of uncontrollable water flowing through the Delta and into the Pacific Ocean. The comparatively static, solid line indicates combined CVP and SWP pumping. The effect of the BiOps pumping restrictions are plain to see—the ability to pump water south is now essentially divorced from the volume of water available in the north. The result of this disconnect is illustrated in Attachment 3. The blue bars compare the volume of water that flowed into the Pacific in 2015 and 2016. The red bars compare the volume of water pumped in the same time frame. Despite there being 350 percent more water flowing through the Delta this year, the Projects were allowed to only capture 50 percent more than last year. It is undeniable that regulation is the significant driver behind chronic water supply shortages; natural drought just exacerbates the already bad situation.

By any measure, 2016 will be a historic year, and likely turning point, for the Projects. For 4 years now we, all of us, have been told that when the rains return to California, so will the water. But that has not happened. Looking forward, it seems unlikely that the decades-long decline in Delta smelt and winter-run salmon populations will suddenly, dramatically, and sustainably reverse absent new management approaches. If that is so, what are the implications for California, the eighth largest economy in the world and producer of about 50 percent of the Nation's fruits, nuts, and vegetables? What are the implications to the financial investment Congress and other have made in the CVP? And what are the implications to the cultural, socio-economic, and environmental conditions of the people once encouraged to settle and develop communities in the Central Valley, a population roughly the size of the state of Colorado?

We are at a critical juncture. Our agricultural and municipal water users have continually adapted to the ever-increasing regulatory demands, becoming among the most efficient users of water in the world. However, continued gains through conservation, reuse, and recycling are not limitless, are extremely costly, and in some cases economically infeasible. The myopic attention on flows over the past quarter century have contributed mightily to the terrible status of several species today. Regulators have too readily seized upon flows in part because it is an easy, tangible, "feel good" change to make. And while virtually every drop of water used for agricultural and municipal purposes must be accounted for, the fastest growing segment of water demand, environmental management, has no such requirement for accountability. Moreover, the prevalent single stressor, single species approach imposed by FWS and NMFS ignores the consistent and pervasive scientific advice that multiple stressors are work therefore comprehensive solutions are necessary if we are to be successful. As an example, habitat restoration has long been identified as an important part of the solution, but progress has been inexcusably slow given the decades listed fish populations have been under stress. Ultimately, better solutions will require better approaches, science, and decisionmaking processes to ensure that we are not the first generation of resource managers that leave both environmental and water supply conditions worse for the next generation. The time is now, the choice is ours and, for many of us, the choice is obvious.

WATER SUPPLY UNCERTAINTY DUE TO DELTA SMELT MANAGEMENT

Population

Delta smelt population indices are at an all-time low, which is a natural cause for concern and the primary driver of fears regarding the potential for extinction. However, while the population indices do tell us about the general trend in Delta smelt abundance, they do not provide us an accurate estimate of actual population. There are several reasons for this. First, the monitoring methods used to measure Delta smelt numbers and distribution are inefficient. A boat can trawl the open water looking for Delta smelt and catch a few or none while feet away, individuals sampling the shore with nets can catch tens, even hundreds, at essentially the same location. Also, Delta smelt are known to reside in regions, such as Cache Slough and the Sacramento Ship Channel, that are not counted in the historical population indices or recent FWS population estimates. In other words, the numbers reflected by both are known to be artificially low. Further, these regions not only routinely harbor significant numbers of Delta smelt but, such as with Cache Slough, also some of the healthiest. While for years there has been broad agreement that the current monitoring practices are inefficient and in need of modernization, change has been inexcusably slow.

Extinction concerns should be further moderated by two other considerations. First, work completed earlier this year by U.C. Davis used genetics based measures to assess the effective population size of Delta smelt. The findings are promising and demonstrate that the effective population size of Delta smelt as of the 2014 year class is above the threshold where fitness related genetic diversity is expected to be lost. The implication of the genetic diversity and the effective population size information is that a large number of Delta smelt remain in the San Francisco Estuary system. However, the current disparity between FWS Delta smelt abundance indices and the effective population size is a concern as it may indicate existing monitoring programs will have difficulty adequately representing Delta smelt abundance, distribution or habitat needs. Second, there are two Delta smelt conservation hatcheries, the U.C. Davis Fish Conservation and Culture Laboratory (FCCL) in Byron, California and the U.S. Fish and Wildlife Service's Livingston Stone National Fish Hatchery located at the base of Shasta Dam near Shasta Lake City, California. These facilities exist to raise Delta smelt as a back-up or "refuge" population to insure against extinction. These Delta smelt also represent an untapped resource, as they could be used to conduct field research to improve our very limited understanding of suitable Delta smelt habitat and/or as brood stock to assist in the recovery of the wild population. Unfortunately, current FWS policy prohibits use of these fish beyond the hatchery, so for the vast majority, they are simply reared to be discarded at the end of their 1-year life span. We should be able to do better with our multi-million dollar annual investment.

Incidental Take Level and 2016 Winter Operations

Generally, an Incidental Take Level is the number of a listed species that a regulatory agency anticipates will be taken by the normal, permitted activity of an action agency. For 2016, the FWS calculated an ITL of 56 adult Delta smelt and 392 juveniles for the combined CVP and SWP pumping operations, which supplies water to roughly 2 out of 3 Californians. How the ITL is both calculated and managed raises significant concerns. First, the ITL is unreasonably low. This is in part due to its reliance on the artificially low abundance index numbers. But, it is also because the most recent formula developed and implemented by FWS this year excludes a significant portion of the historical take data largely related to average water-year types. Essentially, the center of the take bell curve was ignored. What remains are the extremes, either really dry years when pumping and turbidity are low anyway, or very wet years when OMR's reverse flow is low because of high San Joaquin River inflow. Under either condition, historical take is generally low. So, by only including outlying years with historically low take, the current ITL formula produces a number much lower than what would reasonably be expected under normal pumping operations. Whether this approach was an explicit policy choice, or a de facto one resulting from choices made by those who created the formula, is unclear. What is clear is that it is not a science issue, and, if left unresolved, will continue to artificially constrain California's water supply, potentially for years to come.

The second, and perhaps more significant, concern with the ITL is its psychological effect. With the adult abundance index at an all-time low, and an all-time low ITL, the handful of biologists making day-to-day operational decisions have begun viewing the ITL as a number to avoid rather than one to be expected, as demonstrated in Smelt Working Group notes stating that zero salvage should be considered a requisite to increased pumping. Under normal conditions, an ITL will be exceeded periodically and the process thereafter is to reconsult, which has happened with adult DS in the past. Under today's conditions, the fear of reconsultation is great, in part because the fear of extinction is overblown. When the Projects asked FWS what would happen *this* year if the ITL of 56 fish was exceeded, the answer was that OMR, and therefore pumping, would likely be constrained to the bare minimum of −1,250 cfs for the remainder of the adult spawning period, perhaps months. The apprehension that results prompts the CVP and SWP operators to take actions to not just minimize, but avoid, their otherwise lawful, permitted level of take. The resultant water supply cost due to lost pumping between January and March 2016, was approximately 820,000 acre-feet (Attachment 4) with no demonstrable benefit to Delta smelt abundance. That is enough water to serve about 1.6 million households for a year, to farm approximately 270,000 acres of crops, and to produce billions dollars of economic activity. In the end, the resultant socio-economic harm is a policy choice, not a scientific question, and yet for the most part, the harmful results stem from the unchecked opinions of a few state and Federal biologists.

If the purpose of a BiOp is to avoid jeopardy and adverse modification of critical habitat, what information has the FWS developed to demonstrate the operational constraints imposed upon CVP and SWP operations over the last 9 years are achieving those goals? Regrettably, there is none and, rather than that fact leading to a wholesale re-evaluation of how and what is being done to protect and recover Delta smelt, the FWS is proposing a more of the same strategy. The mantra today has become every fish matters but, only if they *may* be affected by the Projects. In the meantime, the FWS continues to do little to address the multitude of other stressors that independent scientists have been telling us for decades, ignore at your own peril. Delta smelt were listed nearly 25 years ago, what has FWS done to address other stressors? What other BiOps, ITLs, permits, and restrictions has FWS imposed on activities beyond the Projects? What explains the willingness of FWS to take, in a single day, at a single location, the number of adult Delta smelt equivalent to the total allowed the Projects for the entire year? The response would likely be concern about entrainment in the south Delta in general, not just salvage. But, what evidence demonstrated this was occurring? The January through March Spring Kodiak Trawl data clearly demonstrates that the vast proportion of Delta smelt were along the Sacramento River between Suisun Marsh and the Sacramento Ship Channel (Attachment 4), far to the north, consistent with historical distribution. The Smelt Working Group's biologists' response is that lack of Delta smelt in the monitoring data is not evidence of their absence, and that may be, but it certainly says something about the relative proportion at risk and the disproportionate regulatory response to their protection.

Ultimately, what this years' experience demonstrates is how far we have veered from the use of best available science and the blurred distinction between science and policy choices. Multi-billion dollar decisions impacting millions of lives and numerous public policy initiatives are being made in isolation by a handful of individuals based upon conjecture and belief, not science. At what point does unbridled discretion become an abuse of authority? Or, is this the new normal for California and all that depend upon the CVP?

Summer Flow Enhancement

In what can only be described as a Hail Mary, the FWS is proposing it's most desperate action yet, increasing summer outflow in the hope it may produce more Delta smelt. Unfortunately, the proposal as described in various meetings—it is not yet documented—does not appear to be supported by the weight of scientific evidence. Our current understanding is that the FWS is pressing Reclamation to acquire between 80,000 and 115,000 acre-feet of water to augment Delta outflow in August and September of 2016, and between 200,000 and 300,000 acre-feet of additional outflow from July through September in 2017 and 2018. The intent is to move "X2", the location in the Delta where salinity is at two parts per thousand, further west in the hope that this new location will somehow benefit the population. The cost to move X2 is significant, both in terms of water and money. Recently, Reclamation identified the activities from which it would take $10,880,000 from existing projects, including from the Battle Creek Salmon and Steelhead Restoration Project, one of the largest cold-water anadromous fish restoration efforts in North America, and refuge water supplies, which are not only an already unmet statutory obligation, but a vital resource in the protection of migratory birds protected under Migratory Bird Treaty Act of 1918 as well as management of numerous other endangered species. Furthermore, while the FWS has been clear that this proposed action is outside the bounds of the BiOp, and therefore should be a non-reimbursable cost to the CVP, Reclamation has yet to insure that the costs that may be incurred will not be rebilled to CVP contractors.

In putting forth its proposal, FWS has not only ignored the best available science but also the Administration's commitment to transparency, participation, and collaboration. The published literature indicates that Delta Smelt abundance is unrelated to summer outflow, the location of X2, or the volume of low salinity habitat. It also suggests that Delta smelt would not move from one location to another because of a change in the location of X2. And if they did, published field studies demonstrate they would likely leave superior habitat like that in the Cache Slough region of the Sacramento River, where most of them are currently located, for some of the poorest quality habitat, which is in Suisun Bay. In other words, the proposed flow augmentation could actually further harm Delta smelt, though none of the potential adverse effects of this discretionary action have been analyzed. It is just assumed the benefits will outweigh the consequences. Rather than risking millions of dollars on this ill-conceived idea, the biological benefit of which will likely never be measured, we should invest in research and actions that could yield tangible results, such as understanding the biological mechanisms driving Delta smelt declines.

WATER SUPPLY UNCERTAINTY DUE TO WINTER-RUN MANAGEMENT

Nine months into the water year, CVP and SWP contractors finally have a salmon temperature management plan. However, while the plan allows for operations much closer to those originally approved by NMFS on March 31, 2016, it also contains a number of conditions and off-ramps that if triggered would rapidly result in decreased releases from Shasta Reservoir and potentially severe water supply disruptions throughout the Central Valley. In early May, Reclamation and NMFS learned that Shasta Reservoir was warmer than expected, thus NMFS informed Reclamation that the March 31 concurrence was no longer supportable and the effort to formulate a new plan was initiated. Over the course of nearly 2 months,

NMFS, the California Department of Fish and Wildlife, the State Water Resource Control Board, the California Department of Water Resources, and Reclamation worked diligently, and insularly, to produce another acceptable plan, which was finally approved on June 28, 2016. While agreement was welcomed, the process for developing the plan and disproportionate attention given to a single biological stressor is cause for great worry going forward.

Generally, the salmon life cycle has a number of important stages: the egg-to-fry stage, when they are most sensitive to temperature, the juvenile stage when they will attempt to migrate down the Sacramento River to rear in the Delta and ocean, the adult stage when they mature in the ocean for about 2½ years, and finally the adult migration back home to spawn so that the cycle can begin all over again. At each step, there are a number of manageable factors that affect the survival of salmon. The Herculean temperature management planning effort focused thousands of staff hours, nearly a hundred model scenarios, and untold policy conversations to wrestle a decision about whether another nearly 400,000 acre-feet of water should be taken from water users to improve the predicted temperature related survival of winter-run salmon from 94 percent to 95 percent. All the while, relatively little was, or is, being done to address the estimated 75 percent predation related mortality that will occur as the juvenile salmon migrate downstream to the sea, or the near 20 percent harvest related mortality that will occur as a result of commercial and recreational fishing in the ocean. For the few that successfully survive the journey, other factors will affect their reproductive success, such as the quality and availability of suitable spawning gravel and habitat conditions in the river. Typically, only about 0.05 percent of the eggs laid in the river will survive to maturity at age 3 and successfully reproduce the next generation to complete their lifecycle. For 2016, the work done to develop the water temperature management plan predicts that temperature-related mortality for winter-run salmon to be 5 to 6 percent, which means over 94 percent of the expected mortality will be resulting from other causes.

Is temperature related survival a vital step in the salmon lifecycle? Of course, but it is not the only vital step; successful temperature management does not always translate into a high number of mature adults returning to spawn. The reality is, if we get survival at one life stage perfect, and ignore other sources of mortality, we fail. The fact that winter-run salmon stocks, along with other Central Valley salmon, have continued to decline so significantly over the past several decades is a clear and strong indicator that the current management approach of focusing disparately on only a few select stressors has not proven to be effective. So, while we should be concerned about the poor temperature related survival of the past 2 years, we should not be surprised by the overall low abundance of winter-run salmon. Until we implement a comprehensive approach to their care, winter-run, along with other salmon, will continue to suffer.

While efforts are underway to establish more collaborative forums to assess the state of knowledge regarding Central Valley salmonids and to provide a basis for designing and implementing improved management actions, the pace is too slow and the level of Federal effort disproportionate to the problem. Discussions among public water agencies, environmental and fisheries organizations, and state and Federal agencies demonstrate a willingness and ability to collaborate on comprehensive solutions. These discussions have identified a diverse set of potential management actions, such as spawning gravel augmentation and habitat improvements, reducing predation, improving hatchery management, implementing a mark-select harvest program to reduce commercial and recreational fishing impacts to wild and listed salmon, improved methods for transporting and releasing salmon, among others. In 2014 and 2015, CVP contractors worked with Reclamation to make available a quarter billion dollars of water to augment temperature management potential. But to fully realize the potential of Federal, state, and local government and private partnerships, NMFS must dedicate the resources necessary to help develop, and ultimately permit, these multi-stressor solutions.

RECOMMENDATIONS

We are upon another historic turning point in the management of listed species and the Projects. The choices made over the coming months will impact California, the Nation, and beyond, probably for decades. On one hand, we can continue down the path established by the FWS and NMFS over a quarter century ago: single species, single stressor management, insular science and process void of experimentation, balance, or accountability, and failing to protect, much less recover, the species. Or, we can embark on a new path, one that is collaborative, transparent, comprehensive and far more likely to produce beneficial results for listed species and the people who both care for their protection yet depend upon the Projects' for an affordable, reliable, and sufficient water supply.

We understand that Interior and the California Department of Water Resources are currently working on a framework for furthering an array of short-term actions aimed at helping smelt. This is helpful as it may bring some order to this very chaotic regulatory and operating environment. To inform this process and others needing guidance and oversight, we offer the following recommendations. It is not the aim of the San Luis & Delta-Mendota Water Authority to eliminate or undermine environmental protection. On the contrary, it is our interest to develop, implement, and support *effective* environmental protection.

Need for Transparency

On his first day in office, President Obama signed the Memorandum on Transparency and Open Government to express his administration's commitment toward improving government openness, efficiency, and effectiveness through transparency, participation, and collaboration. Unfortunately, little of the potential of this commitment has been realized by the FWS and NMFS. The examples of concern above were born in insular processes followed by choice, not necessity. If public water agencies and the people we serve are to suffer the consequences of the regulations imposed upon them, they also deserve to know throughout the formulation process the need, scientific basis, policy trade-offs, and anticipated outcomes of the proposed action. Sadly, this level of transparency, and the accountability that should accompany it, is not present today. This should change.

Need for Collaboration

Despite their best efforts, the Federal and state regulatory and resource agencies have not been able to adequately protect listed species nor provide sufficient water supply to millions of Californians. This reality is due to a number of factors: limited budgets, lack of resources, legal authorities, and capabilities, among them. In order to ensure better outcomes going forward, Federal and state agencies should partner with public water agencies, and other entities, committed to and capable of expanding efforts to address the myriad of problems we face today. Public water agencies provide a unique, largely untapped, resource to help address the environmental and operational concerns affecting management of listed species and the Projects. Public water agencies hold a distinct position in California's water resource management chain, serving as intermediary between the Federal and state agencies and as fiduciaries to the tax and rate payers that both fund and rely upon our collective services. Public water agencies also have specialized operational knowledge, modeling and scientific capabilities, a unique concern in the policies, practices, and outcomes of Federal and state government actions, and extraordinary expertise and resources to bring to bear.

An example of an ongoing scientific and management oriented collaborative effort is the Collaborative Science and Adaptive Management Program, or CSAMP. It includes representatives from Federal and state fish and wildlife and water supply agencies, public water agencies, and environmental organizations. While this forum was born from the litigation over the 2008 and 2009 FWS and NMFS biological opinions and was created to help address the most controversial science questions related to the BiOps in an inclusive and collaborative manner, it continues to work voluntarily today with the aim of minimizing divergent views and potential conflicts associated with the science used to inform future opinions. Over the last 3 years, the effort has identified key knowledge gaps and disagreements in our understanding of Central Valley salmonids and provided recommendations to resolve them, and has begun a series of analyses examining questions related to the impact of Project operations from entrainment and fall outflow on Delta smelt. While initial progress was slow, trust and a strong collegial work environment has emerged. Unfortunately, both recent processes to develop the FWS summer flow proposal and the NMFS re-evaluation of the salmon temperature management plan chose to ignore the CSAMP collaborative approach; rather, employing the traditional insular method. Much of the controversy that exists today regarding these two proposals could have been minimized, and perhaps avoided, if a collaborative approach like CSAMP had been utilized from the outset. If the better outcomes we are all seeking are to be achieved, a better process to develop the science and management actions and evaluate their performance is necessary.

Related to collaboration is the attendant need to implement true adaptive management programs. While the BiOps talk about adaptive management, it is not effective adaptive management in that it provides no formal, structured path for ongoing stakeholder participation in the questioning and testing of hypotheses to refine or reject management actions based upon the scientific evidence. What is in place current has basically been used by the FWS and NMFS to impose stricter regulatory criteria or thresholds unilaterally, without any monitoring or assessment of the actions biological efficacy. As with investing, we should not adopt a set it and forget it approach to environmental management.

Need to Understand Cause and Effect

For decades now, numerous independent scientists and peer review panels have cautioned against too much reliance upon statistical correlations and have recommended we focus instead on researching cause and effect relationships. Correlations can be misleading because they do not always reflect the actual cause-and-effect relationships or the underlying mechanisms. Absent causal information, it is difficult to predict how changes in an environmental variable can effect changes in the population of a species. By better understanding the biological mechanisms at work, we will develop management actions that are both more efficient and effective. Yet, despite overwhelming agreement to the contrary, the FWS yet again proposes a management action based upon a very weak statistical relationship. The current FWS proposal to augment summer Delta outflow hinges on the idea that Delta smelt abundance is somehow linked to the location of X2 (the location in the Delta where salinity is at 2 ppt) in the western Delta. X2 is the poster child of the cause and effect warning.

From its very onset in 1996, the "so-called 'fish-X2' relationships", as it used to be referred to, was recognized as being a "rather crude management tool" by the Interagency Ecological Program, which stated, "More precise influence on these species in terms of quantity or timing of outflow would be desirable for efficient management. In addition, the potential influence of alternative or complementary management actions is difficult to determine from these [statistical] relationships." The U.S. Geological Survey offered similar caution observing, "Significant scientific uncertainty remains, however, about the specific linkages between salinity [i.e. X2] and fish species abundance and about how the aquatic ecosystem within the Delta and Suisun Bay might respond to changes in water flow management. Information is also needed about the relationships between river flow and . . . the effects of contaminants both in the water, and associated with suspended and bottom sediments [i.e. causal mechanisms]." In 2006, an independent science review panel report examining the then occurring Pelagic Organism Decline remarked, "More generally, in using historical data to infer the effect of an environmental variable on a biological population, it is important to go beyond simply attempting to establish a correlation between the environmental variable and abundance. Instead, inference should be based on an understanding of the direct effect of the environmental variable on population dynamics (e.g., on one or more vital rates) and how this direct effect would be reflected in abundance." And again, just months ago speaking before the State Water Resources Control Board, Lead Scientist of the Delta Science Program, Dr. Cliff Dahm stated when summarizing key take home messages from the "Flows and Fishes in the Sacramento-San Joaquin Delta" report, "The first one is that moving forward, we really need to focus more on cause and effect relationships, not just correlations, because correlations can sometimes be spurious."

For more than 20 years, scientists working on Bay-Delta fishery issues have overly relied upon statistical correlations to establish environmental management regulations, and after 20 years, billions of dollars spent, millions of acre-feet dedicated, and untold socio-economic disruption, the species we have sacrificed so much for are in worse shape than ever. We cannot roll back the clock and recover 20 years of lost research opportunity, but we also do not need to spend another 20 years following the same failed path. Rather than spend the tens of millions of dollars necessary to purchase water for the FWS summer X2 outflow action, the effects of which we will likely never be able to determine, we should invest in research that will bring about tangible results, actionable information, and much needed efficacy toward advancing species management.

Need to Experiment

Many of the regulations steadfastly in place today began as simply hypotheses—just ideas really, many without much scientific foundation or certainty. As originally written by scientists, these hypotheses usually contain copious caveats with words like "may" and "should," error bands, confidence intervals, and recommended actions to test the hypothesis so that it may be refined or rejected based upon the empirical information. This process is generally referred to as the "scientific method" and it has served us well for hundreds, if not thousands of years. Enter the regulators. Well intended as they may be, their job is to build boxes. Boxes do not have windows or doors; the walls are rigid and boundaries certain. Into these boxes regulators place the hypotheses, but since the hypotheses are flexible by definition, they must be changed, specific thresholds selected, appropriate caveats replaced with words like "will" and "shall," and the scientific method as an ongoing process is supplanted by the process of regulatory policy choices. If the policy choices are controversial, regulators often defend them by presenting false choices and certainty. For example, under the FWS BiOp we are told that the Projects' pumping operations jeopardize Delta smelt, therefore restrictions on OMR must be established and Projects' pumping cannot exceed a specified rate. There is no evidence that entrainment of Delta smelt by the Projects has a population level effect. Notwithstanding, we are told that minimizing entrainment by imposing the OMR restriction is the only way to avoid jeopardy, the false choice, and that −5,000 cfs OMR is an absolute threshold, the false certainty. Cementing the outcome, ongoing monitoring of the effectiveness of the policy choices and/or an adaptive management process for implementing and testing alternative management actions is rarely a part of the regulatory requirement. Then, if after years of implementation the chosen actions fail to produce discernable results, the false certainty present at promulgation is replaced by equivocation about the complexity of the system and challenges of demonstrating biological benefit. Meanwhile, the resultant sacrifices by water users continue unabated. Such is the history of the CVP and SWP biological opinions.

If we are to have effective environmental protections and balance various policy objectives, we must be able to test and critically evaluate the performance of the regulations currently in place. As an example, restrictions on the OMR net reverse flow have been in effect for 9 years. This regulation has effectively divorced the water supply for two-thirds of Californians residing south of the Delta from their water sources in the northern Sierras. Practically, the OMR restriction limits CVP and SWP pumping to about one-third of the Projects' physical capacity, and to about 40 percent of what would be allowed under the state's Water Quality Control Plan. As a result, the Projects have pumped less water throughout this 9-year period than in any other equivalent time frame in Projects' history. Yet, despite the significant cuts to pumping, Delta smelt and winter-run salmon have continued to decline, raising questions as to the effectiveness of the OMR regulation. In addition, the analyses that supports the hypothesis that increasing negative OMR can result in increased fish salvage and reduced survival also demonstrate that high negative OMR can result in little and even no salvage. So, apparently other factors are at work. However, when public water agencies have requested testing pumping rates higher than allowed under the BiOps, the FWS and NMFS have disapproved. Essentially, the rationale is that an experiment to test the efficacy of operational limits set under the BiOps is not allowable because it would result in operations that exceed the limits set by the BiOps. Under this logic, we can never change the existing standard because we can never test a greater alternative management threshold.

Another example is a calendar restriction on pumping based upon a proportion of San Joaquin River inflows (Inflow:Export ratio) in the April and May time frame under the NMFS BiOp. Essentially, in the BiOp NMFS states that what is needed to improve outmigration for listed steelhead is greater San Joaquin River flow, however, since they were unable to achieve that via the BiOp, they chose to implement a pumping restriction instead. In recent years there have been experimental survival studies conducted in the San Joaquin River and Delta that have not detected a relationship between exports and survival of juvenile steelhead. Studies conducted with salmon have produced similar results. Unfortunately, although the available steelhead survival studies had variable pumping rates, no steelhead survival studies have tested export effects outside the boundaries of the NMFS BiOp, so they do not tell us if a greater pumping limit would also be appropriate. In order to truly assess the efficacy of this regulation, and others, in order to improve pumping potential, experimentation over a wide range of conditions is necessary; otherwise, we can be assured that when future storms come, we will not be able to capture that water either.

Need for Comprehensive Solutions

The desperation behind so many of today's regulatory proposals stem from the natural concern regarding the current status of Delta smelt and winter-run salmon. But too often, we are asking the wrong questions. How are the projects causing the problem, to which we have invested millions, as opposed to what is the problem, which is a very different, far more important questing that we have invested little. If we are to extricate ourselves from the species abundance, water supply death spiral we are in, we must finally begin to develop and implement comprehensive and coherent approaches that begin to address the multiple stressors we know are at work. Clearly, the current management approaches are not working but we have an

33

opportunity before us to embrace a more diverse set of management actions over a larger spatial scale. We have the technical ability, but do we have the will?

Need to Address Needs in the Near Term

For about a decade now, the Projects and regulatory agencies have been generally focused on two areas, immediate needs, as in today's fire drill, or long-term planning, such as storage or conveyance projects, like California Water Fix, that may go into operation a decade or more from now. What has been left out is everything in between. As examples, the habitat restoration called for in the BiOps, if implemented with the same zeal as water supply cuts, could have already been providing us important information, and potentially more fish, today. Hatchery improvements and a mark-select fishery could yield the fish industry improved harvest in a few short years. Predator hot spot removal could begin at any time and provide immediate relief from a significant form of fish mortality. It is not a lack of good ideas standing in our way; rather, it is a lack of will, resources, and leadership. We know what to do, we just have to go and do it.

CONCLUSION

In the end, "Changing Demands and Water Supply Uncertainty in California" is less about how agriculture and municipalities are using water, we have been doing more with less for decades. Rather, it is about the huge increase in environmental water demand over the last quarter century due to unbridled regulation. But, unlike agricultural and municipal usage which must account for the use and ensure the benefit of each drop, environmental usage undergoes no such scrutiny. On the contrary, its benefit is simply assumed. Looking forward, it is incumbent upon us as servants of the public to question the efficacy of the water, money, and human sacrifice demanded for species management. Clearly some of what we are doing today is wholly ineffective, and yet it continues. We must reassess our approaches, broaden participation, enlist stakeholder support, and demand accountability in decision-making if we are to achieve better results. I appreciate the opportunity to testify before you today and would be happy to answer any questions. Thank you.

ATTACHMENT 1

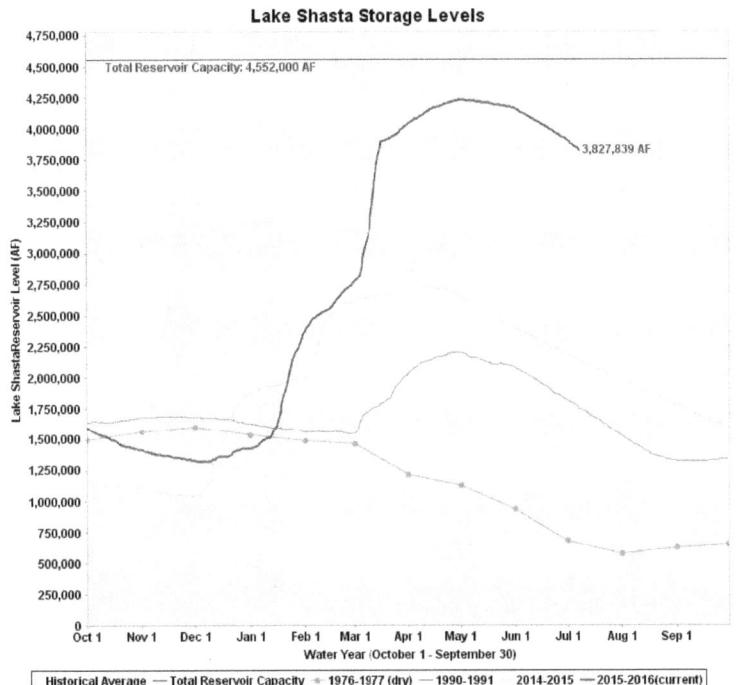

ATTACHMENT 2

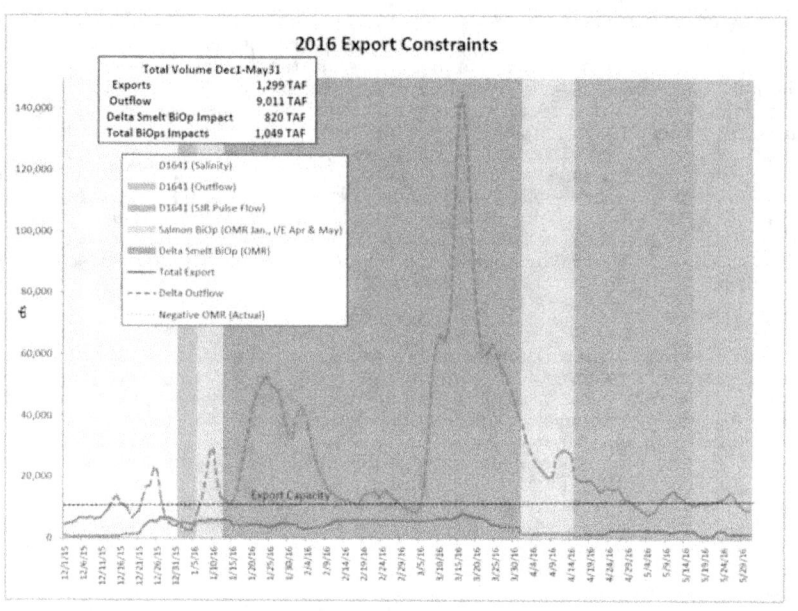

ATTACHMENT 3

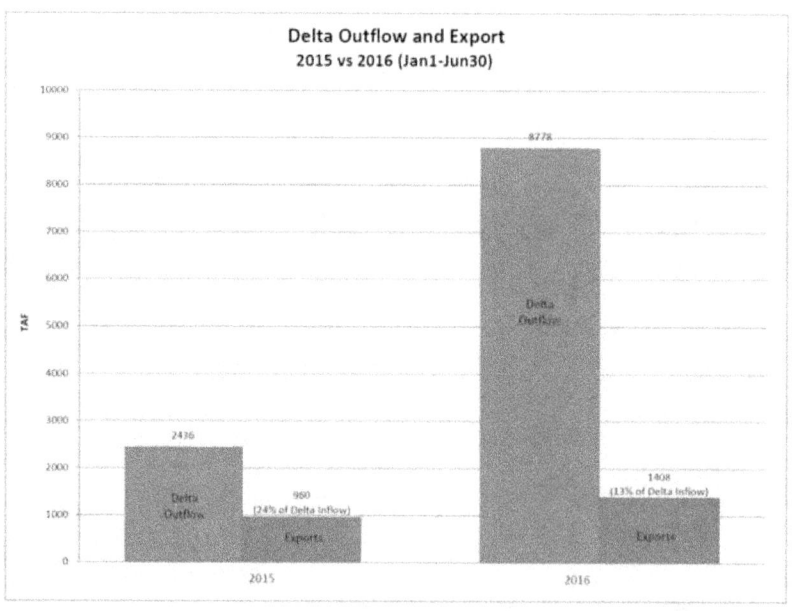

ATTACHMENT 4

Spring Kodiak Trawl Survey #1 of 2016
Sex Ratios of Male and Female Delta Smelt
(1/11/2016 - 1/14/2016)

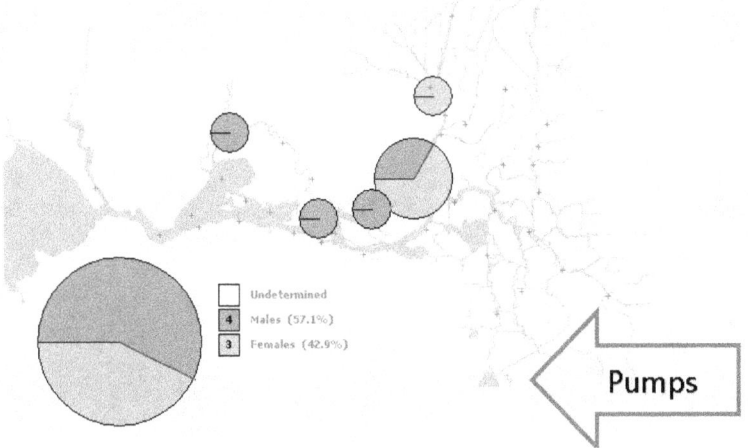

Spring Kodiak Trawl Survey #2 of 2016
Sex Ratios of Male and Female Delta Smelt
(2/8/2016 - 2/11/2016)

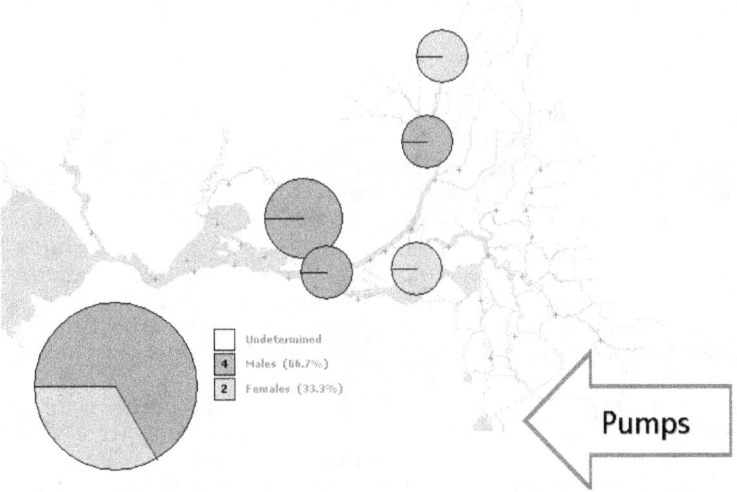

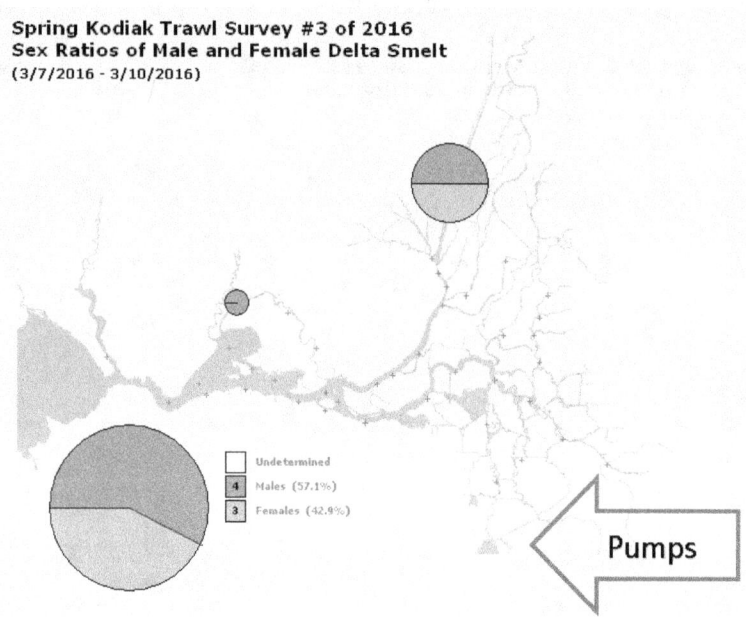

Spring Kodiak Trawl Survey #3 of 2016
Sex Ratios of Male and Female Delta Smelt
(3/7/2016 - 3/10/2016)

Dr. FLEMING. OK. Thank you.

Thank you for your testimonies. We will now go to questioning. I yield myself 5 minutes for questioning.

This question is to Mr. Sutton and Mr. Azhderian. The state of Louisiana depends on healthy fisheries for part of its economy. As Mr. Borck testified, there are parts of California that depend on adequate seafood harvest as well, but both of you questioned whether increased flows actually lead to more fish, particularly with the Fish and Wildlife Service's latest flow proposal on the Delta smelt. I have a lengthy report from Dr. Scott Hamilton that studies the proposed smelt flows, and it concludes that "they do not demonstrate that increasing outflows is a viable method of increasing the abundance of adult Delta smelt."

What I have heard from you is that billions of gallons have been diverted from farms and communities and billions of taxpayer and rate payer dollars have been spent, but that fish levels keep on declining. All of this begs the question of whether the Federal Government's plans are actually working and whether they should be repeated in light of that failure.

So here is the question: What metrics are in place to determine whether more water equals more fish? Mr. Sutton, Mr. Azhderian.

Mr. SUTTON. Well, maybe the question would be better sent to the Federal agencies. We have struggled on looking at this. The metrics, it is hard to say, but in response to your question, I do want to point out, since 1992, the passage of CVPIA, increased implementation of biological opinions have gotten more and more restrictive. We have seen our water supply get more and more regulated, repurposed to other uses, inability to be able to divert that water, to points that we have never seen. We have made it through other droughts. In the late 1980s, early 1990s, and mid-1970s, we saw droughts that were as bad as what we are experiencing, they are very close to what we are experiencing now. Since that time, we have spent well over a billion and a half dollars in ecosystem restoration.

Dr. FLEMING. Mr. Sutton, I hate to interrupt you, but I have more questions.

Mr. SUTTON. I am sorry. OK.

Dr. FLEMING. And the question is metrics, and from what I am taking from your response——

Mr. SUTTON. I don't have those metrics.

Dr. FLEMING. You don't have any.

Mr. SUTTON. What we know, the fish are not recovering——

Dr. FLEMING. OK.

Mr. SUTTON [continuing]. And we are harming farmers as well.

Dr. FLEMING. Mr. Azhderian?

Mr. AZHDERIAN. Mr. Chairman, in terms of monitoring programs that aim to clearly demonstrate if the use of water is affecting beneficially a change in fish, there aren't deliberate and concerted efforts to measure it that way. We really have the abundance indices to rely upon.

What we have seen, for example, since the implementation of the Fish and Wildlife, National Marine Fisheries Services BiOps and the constraints on pumping, is far less pumping occurring and fish declines co-occurring. And millions of acre-feet have been dedicated to environmental management purposes——

Dr. FLEMING. So, again——

Mr. AZHDERIAN [continuing]. Over the last several decades, and the fish have not responded.

Dr. FLEMING. So, you are not even able to impute in any way that, but just anecdotally, that there is an increase in fish as a result of more water. I mean, I am a physician and a businessman. Everything we do, we measure for effectiveness. So it does not make sense to me to be spending literally billions of dollars and not even checking to see if there are any good results of that.

Now, Mr. Borck primarily blames the infrastructure as the problem. What is your response to that and what is your alternative to helping the fish?

Mr. AZHDERIAN. Clearly, the fishing industry is hurting, as the agricultural community is, and no one wants to see that.

In terms of improving salmon abundance, there are a number of methods that we could be employing. We could be improving hatchery production, we could be improving harvest practices, we could be implementing mark select fisheries to better protect the wild stocks and better identify the hatchery fish, making it safer for fishermen to do their harvest. There are a lot of things that could be done, that are done in the Pacific Northwest in Oregon and Washington, that are not done in California for whatever reason.

Mr. SUTTON. I would add, the NMFS action has been solely focused on temperature and getting the young to come out, and that is an important part. The degree we were talking about is a couple of percent to provide the water that would keep water users from a catastrophic disaster, yet we have done nothing to focus on how that juvenile can get down the river system, get through the Delta and get to the ocean. And focusing on that life stage is just as important. There is a lot of investment that the Sac Valley water users have voluntarily engaged in to try and protect that life. We have to focus on the whole life cycle. We just keep turning the water knob unsuccessfully.

I also want to say the striped bass measure that you guys recently passed, Mr. Denham's bill, thank you. There are other stressors that are just being completely ignored that do not account for taking water away from folks.

And, last, we have to build more storage. We have ignored that for decades. Sites Reservoir is a good answer that can help solve this cold water problem by interacting with Shasta.

Dr. FLEMING. I am running out of time, but it sounds like, to sum it up, we keep doing the same old things, getting the same poor results, but somehow expecting some better results. And it sounds like to me it is time to look at other things.

I now yield to the Ranking Member.

Mr. HUFFMAN. Thank you, Mr. Chairman. The other problem is we keep making the same old claims that have been refuted and debunked time and again. One of them is that these biological opinions and the flow parameters that are driven by them are somehow not based on science.

I will ask our witnesses from the Fish and Wildlife Service and the National Marine Fisheries Service quickly about that. These opinions were challenged in court, correct? And they were upheld by the Federal courts, correct? Then at the behest of those who have continued to criticize them, there was an independent peer review by none other than the National Academy of Science, correct? And they were upheld as being scientifically justified by the highest peer review body in the United States of America, correct?

I would hope that we can move beyond continuing to misrepresent the facts on this important issue.

One thing that should be beyond dispute is that for the last 2 years, the project operators have found flexibility within those biological opinions in order to redirect some water that could have gone to fisheries protections, and instead moved them into water deliveries.

So, Mr. Murillo, I just want to ask if it is true that state and Federal agencies used existing flexibility under the Endangered Species Act to redirect about 1.3 million acre-feet over the last 2 years, and doesn't that show that you have been operating the system to try to find as much flexibility as possible?

Mr. MURILLO. Yes, we have worked with the fisheries the last couple of years to use the flexibility that exists within the biological opinions to move more water to Ag.

Mr. HUFFMAN. One consequence of operating the system with that aggressive flexibility has been fishery impacts, as we have heard from our fisheries agencies. So, I just want to ask the two fisheries agencies here if they would agree with the proposition that that flexibility has in turn caused some harm to the struggling fisheries?

Dr. LOHOEFENER. Thank you for the question, Congressman Huffman. Well, one of the aspects I am proudest of over the last

8 years is the collaboration that has been built between the Bureau of Reclamation, National Marine Fisheries Service, California Department of Water Resources, and California Fish and Wildlife. That collaboration has led today to where we make much wiser decisions, but also to recognize——

Mr. HUFFMAN. But my question is whether that flexibility has resulted in some negative consequence to the fisheries. I need a quick answer, if you could, please.

Dr. LOHOEFENER. Implementation of the biological opinion only minimizes harm, it does not remove harm.

Mr. HUFFMAN. All right. And, Mr. Thom, would you agree with that?

Mr. THOM. I would just say it has shown from the monitoring data for both 2014 and 2015 that the survival rate of winter-run Chinook was very low coming out of the Sacramento system over those 2 years.

Mr. HUFFMAN. One of the things at the heart of our discussion here today is that we are continuing to operate the system very aggressively to try to maximize water deliveries, and one consequence of that with the Bureau's temperature management proposal for Lake Shasta and the Sacramento River, is that if it turns out that you have run the system too hard and you have to cut back deliveries to conserve cold water, there is a whiplash effect on Mr. Sutton and on others. So, I am sympathetic to the testimony that he gives about the lack of certainty and the fact that he has planted crops, he has taken out loans, and he is feeling some potential whiplash if this has to happen. Yet, isn't that a consequence of this philosophy that you run the system as aggressively as you can with zero margin for the fishery, and then if it looks like you are about to hit an extinction problem, you cut back deliveries?

There are others that are proposing that we should actually legislate something like that, that we should only cut back for the smelt when they are found exactly in the right place based on real-time management, which would produce that exact same whiplash effect.

So, I guess I am wondering—I have already heard Mr. Sutton explain why this is not working too well for his farmers, that lack of certainty, but I will ask you, Mr. Borck, how well is it working, the fact that we are operating the system to minimum protections and aggressively, with zero margin for error for the fisheries? How has that been working for the fisheries side of the system?

Mr. BORCK. Does anyone want to buy a boat? It is not working. We have half a season. We have Oregon closed. It is not working.

I don't know what it is going to take, because I am not a scientist, but I can tell you right now what we are doing is not helping the fish, obviously it is not helping the farmers, it is not helping 38 million Californians. What we are doing needs to improve. At the same time, you cannot ignore the fact that you have coastal communities that need those fish to make a living.

Mr. HUFFMAN. Thank you.

Thanks, Mr. Chairman.

Dr. FLEMING. OK. Mr. McClintock is recognized.

Mr. MCCLINTOCK. Thank you, Mr. Chairman.

Mr. Murillo, La Niña conditions now appear likely for this winter, do they not?

Mr. MURILLO. I didn't hear your question, sir.

Mr. MCCLINTOCK. La Niña conditions are building now for this winter. Are we looking at another likely dry winter?

Mr. MURILLO. I don't know for sure what the outcome is.

Mr. MCCLINTOCK. Well, I am told that La Niña usually follows an El Niño, and the forecasts I am seeing are for a very dry winter coming up, or certainly a strong possibility of that. My principal concern is the condition of Folsom Lake Reservoir. The fish agency required that Folsom be drawn down dramatically now so that cold water can be held back at Shasta to adjust river temperatures in the fall. Recreational businesses have already been notified they are going to be closing very early. Some of them are going to be going out of business as a result of these early closures. That is not the principal danger. The principal danger is that we never completed Auburn Dam upriver, so we have no way to replenish Folsom if there is a dry winter, and Folsom is the principal source of water for the city of Roseville and its surrounding communities.

My concern is what contingencies your bureau has made for a dry winter coming up if you are draining Folsom right now for the fish?

Mr. MURILLO. The plan has it that at the end of September, we will have about 300,000 acre-feet in Folsom Reservoir.

Mr. MCCLINTOCK. But that is about a third of its capacity and facing a dry winter with no way to replenish it.

Mr. MURILLO. Yes. Absolutely.

Mr. MCCLINTOCK. Don't you think that that is irresponsible?

Mr. MURILLO. Well, we run the system as a whole. It is a system we run. Folsom is part of that system. One thing that we try to make sure is we try to protect the interests that those stakeholders have in Folsom. That is why we——

Mr. MCCLINTOCK. Well, you are not, because you are ordering the early drainage of that reservoir to meet these fish appease.

Mr. Sutton, the Ranking Member referred to the fact that we do have an historic drought. It seems to me in drought conditions, shouldn't we be more careful to hold back what water remains behind our reservoirs?

Mr. SUTTON. I agree.

Mr. MCCLINTOCK. Have we done so?

Mr. SUTTON. Some of the actions are self-defeating.

Mr. MCCLINTOCK. Well, they are inexplicable.

Mr. SUTTON. Yes.

Mr. MCCLINTOCK. I mean, the fact is Californians made exemplary efforts, they sacrificed their lawns, their gardens, they disrupted their lives, only to turn around and watch the government release billions of gallons of water to adjust river temperatures. I wonder what moral authority is government to demand draconian sacrifices by our people when it treats the remaining water so frivolously.

Mr. Azhderian, a biologist was shaking his head in my office last year, pointing out that in a drought salmon do not enter rivers because the water is too warm and there is not enough of it. He said that by artificially cooling the water through releases and pulse flows, we end up tricking them into doing something their own instincts warn them not to do, and it doesn't end well for them. In fact, we have heard that right now. What are your thoughts?

Mr. AZHDERIAN. I think in looking back over historical changes in weather patterns and in salmon abundance, what you will find is we have large numbers of salmon returning after dry years and we have small numbers of salmon returning after wet years. There is a lot in play after they get through that initial spawning phase.

Is temperature management important? Of course it is, but we have spent months, thousands of hours, working through hundreds of operational scenarios to debate a 1 or 2 percentage point change in temperature-related survival, when what we know on average is 99 percent of the salmon, through one form of mortality or another, are not going to return anyway.

Our point is more about proportion and being able to do things that address the larger contributors to the mortality of salmon, and better managed salmon, to ensure that fishermen can catch a healthy harvest when they need it.

Mr. MCCLINTOCK. Mr. Borck, are we doing enough to supplement salmon populations through fish hatcheries?

Mr. BORCK. I am not a scientist.

Mr. MCCLINTOCK. No. You're a fisherman. But are we doing enough to supplement these salmon populations?

Mr. BORCK. I would say that——

Mr. MCCLINTOCK. The reason I ask is there is a movement to tear down the Iron Gate Dam on the Klamath River. When the Iron Gate Dam is torn out, the Iron Gate Fish Hatchery goes with it. The Iron Gate Fish Hatchery produces 5 million salmon smolts a year. That will all be gone when that dam is torn down.

Do you think that is good public policy for your colleagues in the fishing industry?

Mr. BORCK. I think a healthy environment and a healthy planet are in the best interest——

Mr. MCCLINTOCK. Do you support——

Mr. BORCK. Sir——

Mr. MCCLINTOCK [continuing]. Or oppose——

Mr. BORCK [continuing]. Please let me finish.

Mr. MCCLINTOCK [continuing]. Destroying the fish hatchery? That is a simple question.

Mr. BORCK. I think losing a hatchery for the better good of a river system is good policy.

Dr. FLEMING. The gentleman yields.

Mr. Costa.

Mr. COSTA. Thank you very much, Mr. Chairman. And I want to commend you for holding this hearing, because I think it highlights what really is the situation in California, and that is a broken water system. The testimony and the questions, I think, all point out to the difficulty of a saying that I think aptly describes what we are dealing with, and that is, continuing to do what we have always done and expect different results, that is a definition of insanity, and that is what we are doing here by this additional flow that has taken place through the summer runs.

Mr. Lohoefener, I really commend your efforts over the years and your service to our country and your efforts to try to solve problems. Let me ask you, this summer outflow requirement—and certainly I think U.S. Fish and Wildlife Service ought to be combined with NMFS, that was a point that was made earlier. But this summer outflow requirement, is there anything in the biological opinion that requires this to take place?

Dr. LOHOEFENER. Thank you for the question, Congressman Costa. The current biological opinion, the 2008 opinion, only addresses outflows for a fall outflow under wet conditions.

Mr. COSTA. So, the answer is no, there is nothing required in terms of summer outflows?

Dr. LOHOEFENER. In terms of summer outflow, there is nothing required in the opinion.

Mr. COSTA. OK. Then, Mr. Murillo, would you describe this action that has taken place this summer as a voluntary action?

Mr. MURILLO. Yes, a voluntary action.

Mr. COSTA. OK. So it is a voluntary action. Now, let me give you some perspective, folks, of what we are talking about, notwithstanding good intentions. And I care about restoring the salmon fisheries. I know salmon fishermen have been impacted, just as farmers in my area have been impacted with hundreds and thousands of acres that have gone fallow, farm communities, farmworkers, $2.7 billion in losses to the agricultural communities in the valley, and thousands and thousands of jobs that have been lost.

Having said that, this action this summer, this is what it does, and correct me if I am wrong, 300,000 cubic feet per second to move a salinity line down to Cache Slough that is several kilometers in length, right? And what we are talking about is 300,000 cfs of tidal influence. So, somehow we are going to use 300 cubic feet per second to move back 300,000 cfs, cubic feet per second, of salinity that flows into the Cache Slough there as a result of the San Francisco-Sacramento Delta. Is that correct, Mr. Murillo? Is that what we are talking about?

Mr. MURILLO. I believe so.

Mr. COSTA. Ren, do you have any disagreement with that?

Dr. LOHOEFENER. The need is for habitat, so we are trying to take the habitat in the——

Mr. COSTA. Absolutely. So, why shouldn't we be focusing on habitat? Why shouldn't we be focusing on nonpoint discharges that put pollutants in the water? Why shouldn't we provide more habitat for the Delta smelt so that they can survive? Why shouldn't we be dealing with a predator control program?

To Mr. Sutton's comment, we are continuing to do what we have always done, which is driving me crazy, maybe no one else is going crazy, and that is that we are using the water knob, and saying, OK, it has not worked so well, it is continuing to decline, yes, the fisheries are declining, but we will continue to do what we have always done.

Does that bother you, Mr. Lohoefener?

Dr. LOHOEFENER. Well, Congressman Costa, as usual, you are right. There are many threats out there: invasive species, both plants and animals, water quality, but unless you keep the habitat you need for the smelt, all those other factors are going to be moot.

Mr. COSTA. But we are not doing the other things.

Dr. LOHOEFENER. We need to keep the water, we need to keep habitat——

Mr. COSTA. I understand, but we are not doing the other things, and you are working with one tool, one arm behind your back. Three-hundred cfs, I maintain, at the end of the day, with no—are there any matrices that you have to show after this effort in July, August, and September, that we are going to be able to weigh it to determine whether or not we have made any difference?

Dr. LOHOEFENER. As I think you know, Congressman, the Delta smelt is definitely on the brink of extinction this year.

Mr. COSTA. No, I understand. That is not my question. My question is, are there any matrices——

Dr. LOHOEFENER. The state has been——

Dr. FLEMING. Mr. Costa——

Mr. COSTA. Excuse me, please. I would like—It is impolite. Please.

Dr. FLEMING. I apologize.

Mr. COSTA. I would like to reclaim the rest of my time.

Dr. LOHOEFENER. The state has been doing surveys for Delta smelt for over 50 years now. We have greatly improved those in the last 10 years. If we see some——

Mr. COSTA. Is there any real-time monitoring that is going to determine the effects or a matrix for the next 3 months?

Dr. LOHOEFENER. I believe if the surveys find Delta smelt still alive this year, then keeping the habitat and some——

Mr. COSTA. But that is not a matrix and that is not a way. You are very good, and I appreciate your ability to avoid answering the question, but the answer is no. There are no matrices that have been developed to determine this particular voluntary, not in the biological opinion, outflow that we are pursuing this summer for what I would state is de minimis, at best, returns.

One quick last question, Mr. Chairman.

Has there ever been a time in the history of the allocation with the Bureau of Reclamation when after good, bad, indifferent, we know we are in drought conditions, in April they make the allocations to the Federal contractors, that 2 months later, they said, you know, we said that in April, but we really didn't mean it, we are going to have to make changes?

Mr. AZHDERIAN. There have been other examples of that, Congressman. In 2013, Reclamation's initial announcement was 25 percent allocation. Shasta storage was over 100 percent of average. In March, Reclamation announced that due to dry conditions they were going to have to deallocate or unallocate 5 percentage points, so they went from a 25 to a 20. Since implementation of sort of the regulatory era, if you will, beginning in 1992, there have been 3 years since that time that CVP Ag. service contractors south of the Delta received 100 percent supply. Hasn't happened since 2006. And there have been three times when the allocations have been reduced on CVP contractors south of the Delta as a result of circumstances for environmental management.

Mr. COSTA. All right. Thank you.

Dr. FLEMING. Mr. LaMalfa.

Mr. LAMALFA. Thank you, Mr. Chairman. Mr. Sutton, we talked about it a little bit already here. I mean it has certainly been one thing that your district and your neighbor districts there had zero allocation, zero in 2014 and 2015. And then to be told when the lake has reached an incredible fullness that you would go out and plant crops, and sometime in May perhaps, after the crops are in the field, the fertilizer has been bought, the tractors have been run, money has been borrowed from the banks, say, oh, wait a minute, you are not going to get the allocation now. I don't even probably have to get the answer as to how devastating that is going to be in the middle of the year. I used to represent that in the state legislature. Mr. Garamendi has the privilege of representing those counties now below Tehama. I have seen the boarded up windows, the closed down tractor and auto dealerships, and the small storefronts. I mean, how devastating would this be to your constituents?

Mr. SUTTON. Thank you for the question. Like I said, not that I want to encourage David to give me zero allocations in the future, but those were trying years, desperate years. But what could have occurred this year, what we have come on the precipice of almost happening, with 8,000 cfs, the initial recommendation from NMFS, they would have had to turn our water off completely, not because the water wasn't there, but we could not divert it because the senior water rights and fishery protections would take the priority. Even the senior water right holders would have suffered greatly. They have been having impacts to their pumps, having to pump water instead, and some folks not able to plant.

Mr. LAMALFA. You mean from wells, well water.

Mr. SUTTON. Well water. Pardon me. Thank you. So what would have happened? I sit as a member of the Glenn-Colusa Farm Production Credit Association that loans out these operating loans to these farmers to plant their crops and get them through harvest to pay that back. Lending institutions, businesses, farmers would have been lost.

Mr. LAMALFA. Let me jump in there. Did you hear the testimony, did you see that on March 22 we had Eileen Sobeck of NOAA here to talk about the levels of Shasta.

Mr. SUTTON. Correct.

Mr. LAMALFA. I asked her point blank, what would it take, how much water would have to be in the lake for you to assure the senior water rights holders, as well as others, that they are going to get their allocation? She said 4.1 million acre-feet, which is somewhere around 95 percent of full or 108 percent of the average over the years. And at that point they started dumping water and the lake only filled to 3.95 million, but that is a different story.

So what does that mean, if the lake has to reach a level of 4.1 million every year, that if it is below that, you are not going to see an allocation? This is what is going to be played in order to have a temperature goal be met in September or October or what have you?

Mr. SUTTON. We are heading on a trajectory that is unsustainable for the CVP if that is where we are at.

Mr. LAMALFA. Mr. Thom, would you address that too, please?

Mr. THOM. I am sorry, could you repeat the question, I am not sure I understand——

Mr. LAMALFA. Well, let me shift gears on that then. Does your agency believe that no winter-run salmon will return to the river in 2017 and 2018 based on the shouting about what the numbers were going out the river during the 3 years previous?

Mr. THOM. Yes, based on the high mortalities in 2014 and 2015 that we saw in the juvenile outmigrants, we expect very few return spawners, very low year classes to come back in those later years.

Mr. LAMALFA. What is the sampling system used to determine that, especially during high flows?

Mr. THOM. The adult fish returning are counted——

Mr. LAMALFA. Counting the outflow.

Mr. THOM. The outflows are used through smolt trapping carried out by the California Department of——

Mr. LAMALFA. How do you smolt trap during high flows?

Mr. THOM. You don't. You actually subsample some of those.

Mr. LAMALFA. Mr. Sutton, would you touch on how that sampling system works in your observation?

Mr. SUTTON. Just from our observations and conversations with NMFS, one frustrating thing about the numbers reported for 2014 and 2015 are those fish move when they get these pulses, the indicator, the environmental indicator to make them migrate downstream, which is flow. When you get that flow, they actually anchor to the Red Bluff—these screw traps to the Red Bluff diversion dam, the facilities that we run there. And in those circumstances, when you imagine most of those fish are moving by, those traps are out of the water.

Mr. LAMALFA. They are not counting the actual fish in the traps——

Mr. SUTTON. They can't.

Mr. LAMALFA. So we don't even have a real sample, do we?

Mr. SUTTON. Not during the primary time that we would imagine they are migrating.

Mr. LAMALFA. During the primary time when most fish would be moving. So we can expect perhaps really great returns in 2017, 2018. We don't really know, do we?

Mr. SUTTON. I don't believe so. And we are certainly hopeful that that is true.

Mr. LAMALFA. Mr. Azhderian, how much water could be in San Luis Reservoir if 110,000 cfs was not running straight out to the ocean during March and they were actually putting that water into the reservoir? Could it be 2 million acre-feet instead of 1 million full?

Mr. AZHDERIAN. It is difficult to say, Congressman, because California's regulatory environment is an onion and there are so many layers.

Mr. LAMALFA. If they were actually pumping, if they were pumping the water, could you have——

Mr. AZHDERIAN. Yes. It certainly should be a lot fuller than it would be today. And I think one of the implications, this was brought up earlier, about the decisions that were made in May and June to change the temperature management plan is the way it affects 2017. As Mr. Sutton had indicated, farmers were out, they were considering purchasing transfer water. Those opportunities were passed on because of anticipating a full San Luis Reservoir in 2017. Now that seems highly unlikely. In fact, there may be a deallocation from 5 percent to zero percent for west side users, and an empty San Luis Reservoir as we roll into next year. So clearly, the impacts of passing on those opportunities only to have the management come in and second-guess——

Mr. LaMALFA. Thank you. Mr. Chairman, I would like to enter into the record, this is a study commissioned by Mr. Scott Hamilton, who is a Ph.D., which would indicate that no relationship between summer flows and summer survival of Delta smelt is indicated by these high flows during the summer.

Dr. FLEMING. Without objection, so ordered.

[The information follows:]

WILL INCREASING DELTA OUTFLOW HELP DELTA SMELT?

Scott Hamilton, Ph.D., Center for California Water Resources Policy & Management

Draft 5/31/16

EXECUTIVE SUMMARY

While the correlations between abundance and estuarine outflow have been well established for some species, there appears to be considerable uncertainty regarding the benefit of outflows for delta smelt. Here we provide a brief overview of the relationship between the abundance of delta smelt and delta flows during various seasons, drawing on previous studies and publicly available data. The conclusions we draw are:

1. There is no correlation between spring flows and abundance in the summer or fall (Kimmerer et al. 2009).

2. A correlation between spring flows and spring abundance since 1995 has been noted (IEP MAST 2015) but this relationship does not persist to the fall (Kimmerer et al. 2009).

3. The available data shows no relationship between summer flows and summer survival (Bullet #3 under "Supporting Information", below).

4. The available data shows no relationship between fall flows and either survival during the fall or subsequent recruitment (Bullet #4 under "Supporting Information").

5. While the theory underlying hypothesized mechanisms between flows and abundance of aquatic species in general is well documented, the importance of these mechanisms for delta smelt, when tested, has not been well supported (Kimmerer 2002a, Kimmerer et al. 2009).

6. Numerous data points exist where measures of fish success are high at low outflows, and low at high outflows. Without understanding the underlying mechanisms, it is possible that increasing flows may adversely impact delta smelt (see e.g. Figure 5 below).

7. There is not sufficient water available from other sources to increase outflows and move the X2 salinity line by more than 1–2 km. Such a minor change in the X2 line is extremely unlikely to make any significant difference for delta smelt and would come at great cost to other beneficial uses.

8. The existing studies and the best available public data, do **not** demonstrate that increasing outflows **is a viable method of increasing the abundance of adult delta smelt**.

Given the uncertainty surrounding the relationship between outflow and impacts on delta smelt, the potential harm to the species and the implications of reallocating water from other beneficial uses, if more flows are to be pursued for the benefit of delta smelt, we would ask that the Collaborative Science and Adaptive Management Program (CSAMP) be asked to examine the science underlying specific flow proposals.

BACKGROUND

- Delta smelt are an endangered fish in California's Sacramento-San Joaquin Delta and Estuary that, for the most part, live for just one year. Listed in 1993, its numbers have declined severely and they now persist at less than 1% of their number at the time of listing.

- The status of delta smelt, as a species, is gauged by calculating "abundance indexes" from several fish surveys in the estuary. An abundance index is intended to provide an indication of how well a species is doing in relative terms but doesn't translate into a specific population size. The best known are the Fall Midwater Trawl (FMWT) Index, summer Tow Net Survey (TNS) Index[1] and the 20-mm Survey Index. The indexes are now at record low levels. The 20-mm Index, for example, has been as high as 39, averages 11, and in 2015 was at 0.3.

- Increased flow could help aquatic species in a variety of ways: spawning habitat area and volume, spawning habitat access, habitat space, predation avoidance through turbidity and shallows access, reduced entrainment, toxics dilution, increased entrapment zone residence time, habitat diversity, more favorable water temperatures, strengthened gravitational circulation, migratory cues, and higher food production (EET 1996, Kimmerer 2002b)

- Increased outflow has been proposed as one measure that might help delta smelt in the Sacramento-San Joaquin Delta because abundance of some other species is correlated with outflow.[2] Outflow if often quantified using "X2" as a metric. X2 designates the location of the 2% bottom salinity (grams of salt per kilogram of seawater) along the axis of the estuary and is measured in km from the Golden Gate Bridge. The lower X2, the higher the outflow. It is a sensitive index of the estuarine community's response to net freshwater inflow.[3]

SUPPORTING INFORMATION

(Bullets correspond numerically with the executive summary)

Spring Flows

1. Kimmerer et al. (2009) studied the relationship between spring X2 and abundance of delta smelt in the summer and fall and found:[4]

   - a statistically significant (p=0.018) positive relationship (abundance increases as spring outflows decrease) in the summer Tow Net Survey for the period 1959–1981,

   - a slight negative but insignificant (p=0.38) relationship in the summer Tow Net Survey for the period 1982–2007,

   - a slight positive relationship but of marginal significance (p=0.14) in the Fall Midwater Trawl, and

   - a slight negative but insignificant (p=0.6) relationship in the Bay Midwater Trawl. That is, Kimmerer showed that spring outflows were either bad for delta smelt or not significant, and, consistent with earlier studies,[5] concluded [6] "**abundance of delta smelt did not vary with X2**".[7]

2. Using 20-mm abundance (representing young fish, as opposed to summer and fall abundance used by Kimmerer et al 2009 and representing older fish) Figure 79 of the IEP MAST (2015) report (reproduced as Figure 1 below) depicts a non-linear relationship between spring X2 and abundance, with abundance increasing as X2 moves westward to 64 km and then abundance decreasing as X2 moves further westward.

---

[1] Also referred to here as the STN Index
[2] Kimmerer et al 2009, IEP MAST 2015
[3] Jassby et al 1995, p.272
[4] As reported in Table 2
[5] Jassby et al (1995), Kimmerer (2002a)
[6] Kimmerer 2009, p.385
[7] Here and in other places throughout this document, balding and underlining is emphasis added in this document and does not occur in the source documents

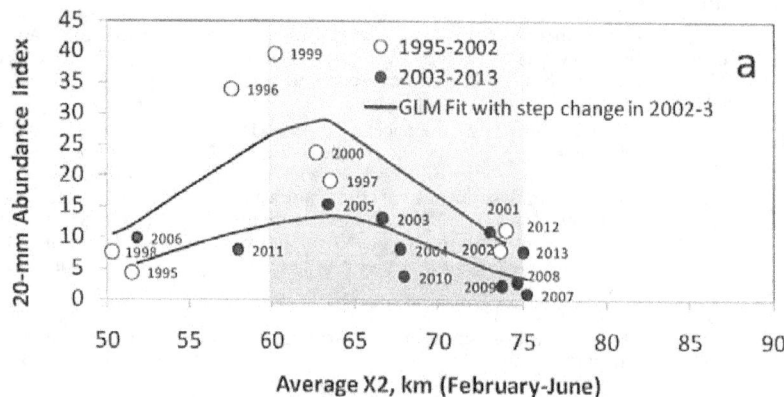

Figure 1. Plots of the Delta Smelt 20 mm survey abundance index as a function of spring (February–June) X2.

Source: IEP MAST (2015), Figure 79.

The IEP MAST report notes[8] that "after 19 years, the 20mm survey now provides barely enough annual abundance data points (indices) to conduct multiple regression analyses with up to two predictor variables." Consequently, we looked to see if the same relationships held with the STN Index (See Figure 2 below). Similar to Figure 1, we observed the response curve has flattened in recent years.

The relationship depicted in Figure 1 provides no guidance as to causality. Indeed the report specifically calls out that "individual and interactive effects of additional factors were not considered in this analysis, but are likely also important."[9]

Even if spring abundance is increased, a comparison of the abundance indexes for the different life stages of delta smelt shows the least correlation between summer and fall. This suggests that even if spring abundance is increased, it is **unlikely to result in an increased number of adults** unless the problems in late summer and fall, which could include factors such as predation and lack of food, are addressed. Consequently, the correlations between spring outflows and 20mm abundance have not been found with abundances in the fall.[10]

---

[8] p.154
[9] p.153
[10] Kimmerer et al 2009

Relationship between Summer Abundance and Spring Flows

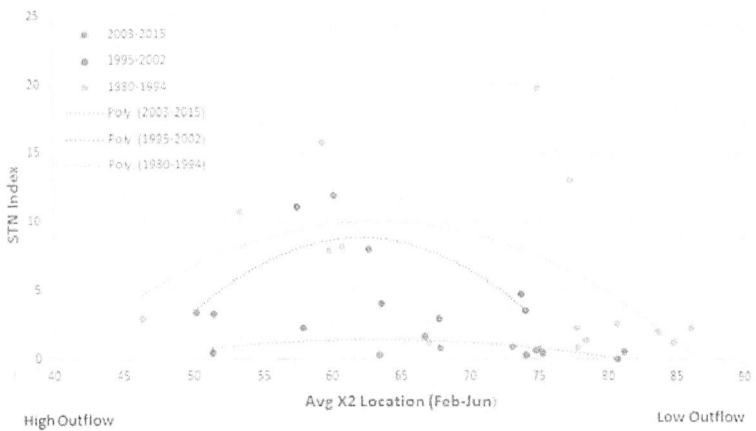

Figure 2. Relationship between summer abundance, as determined by the STN Index, and spring outflow, determined by the average X2 location between February to June, 1980–2015.

Sources: TNS Survey, Dayflow.

A check of the 2003–2013 data from the IEP MAST report (see Appendix A, below) found the nonlinear term to be insignificant and X2 itself to be barely significant (p=0.046) with a coefficient of -0.345. That is, for every 1 km X2 is moved westward, the spring abundance index would increase by 0.345. But there is considerable uncertainty around this coefficient because of the limited number of data points and wide variability in the data—the standard error is 0.146 suggesting the 95% confidence interval for the coefficient is 0.053 to 0.637.

The 20mm survey, which began in 1995, was specifically designed to improve the sampling of young delta smelt. As such, it has advantages over other surveys. However, the period from 1995 to 1999 was wetter than normal. And the last several years, ending in 2015 has been drier than normal. Throughout the period the abundance of delta smelt has generally been decreasing. Delta smelt abundance may be decreasing as a result of hydrology, or it may be decreasing due to some other factor not quantified, but the coincidental trends with hydrology may provide more significance to hydrology than is warranted. Consequently, we suggest that survival and recruitment should be considered, in addition to abundance.

Summer Flows

3. Few studies seem to have been published on the relationship between increased summer outflow and delta smelt abundance. Nobriga et al. (2008) considered long-term trends in summertime habitat suitability finding relationships between summer abundance [11] and salinity, water clarity and water temperature. Flows can influence each of these factors. Nobriga et al (2008) found significant relationships between the presence of delta smelt and the abiotic factors at a regional level but found no significant relationships between any of the water quality variables and delta smelt relative abundance at the estuary-wide level.

A regression analysis of survival from summer to fall using covariates of prior abundance, summer outflow and a trend variable does not indicate summer flows were a significant factor (see Appendix B). Figure 3 below shows the relationship between average X2 location and summer survival.

---

[11] Nobriga et al (2008) used delta smelt data from the summer Tow Net Survey

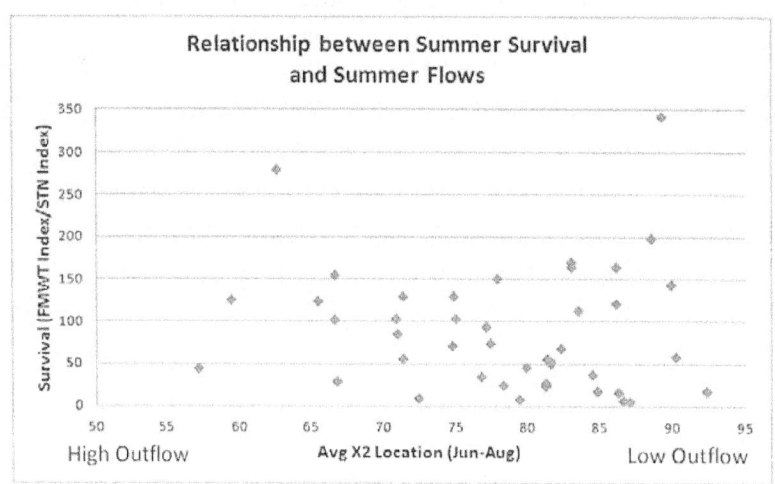

Figure 3. Relationship between summer survival, as determined by the ratio of the FMWT Index divided by the STN Index, and summer outflow, determined by the average X2 location June to August, 1969–2014.

Sources: TNS Survey, FMWT Survey, Dayflow.

Lund et al (2015) depict a delta hydrograph [12] that has flattened over time with lower spring outflows and higher summer outflows. Flows through the Delta, July through September, are now higher than they would have been absent the CVP and SWP due to reservoir reregulation from spring to fall.[13] Has this flatter hydrograph favored non-native species at the expense of native species? Too many factors have changed simultaneously to provide a definitive answer, but providing even more summer outflow would be inconsistent with the natural hydrograph.

Fall Flows

4. MacNally et al. (2010) considered fall abundance of delta smelt and found a relationship with fall outflow but the Odds Ratio was 0.14.[14] An odds ratio greater than 3.2 is needed to conclude substantial evidence, and greater than 10 to conclude strong evidence.

Thompson et al. (2010) found no significant relationship between delta smelt abundance and either spring X2 or autumn X2.

Feyrer et al. (2007) found that salinity (EC at individual stations) during the fall explained 60% of the variation in recruitment (summer abundance compared to prior fall) after the clam invasion (post 1986). However, there appears to be no significant relationship between the monthly average EC at FMWT stations and monthly average X2 in the fall, suggesting that increasing outflow to modify X2 will not necessarily result in a change in the average EC at FMWT stations. Consequently it is difficult to detect a relationship between Fall X2 and recruitment (see Figure 4 below).

A graphical analysis of both survival during the fall and subsequent recruitment suggest **increased outflows during the fall are just as likely to be bad for delta smelt as good for them** (see Figures 4 and 5 below). Some of the higher survival and recruitment actually occurs when fall outflows are low (X2 greater than 80). This should be of particular concern. It suggests that a clear understanding of the underlying mechanisms is not known and that, in a variety of circumstances, increasing flows may decrease abundance.

---

[12] Their Figure 1, p.4

[13] Hutton et al (2015)

[14] It was actually reported by MacNally et al. as "1/7.1" but converted here for ease of comparison

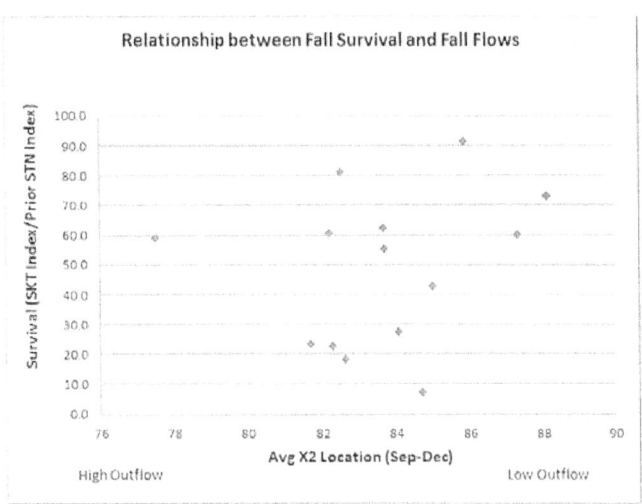

Figure 4. Relationship between Fall Survival, as determined by the SKT Index divided by the prior STN Index, and fall outflow, determined by the average X2 location, September to December, 2001–2015. The survival ratio of winter abundance to summer abundance was used for the survival metric to avoid any overlap with the explanatory variable of flows during the fall.

Source: TNS and SKT Trawls, X2 data from Dayflow. 2002 and 2003 SKT Index was estimated from SKT CPUE.

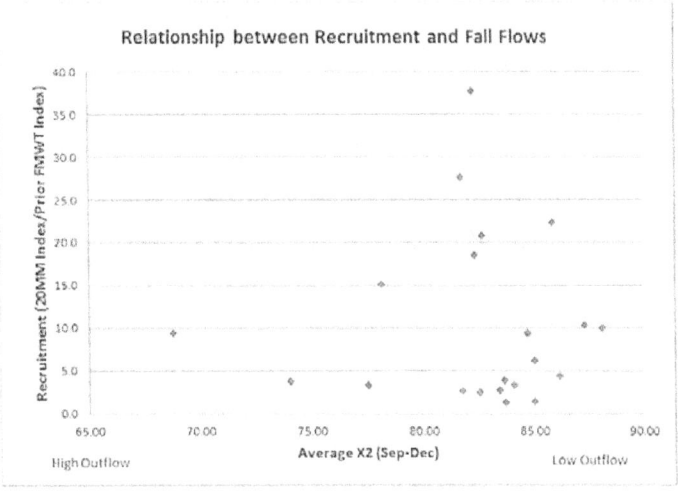

Figure 5. Relationship between recruitment, as determined by 20MM Index divided by the prior FMWT Index, and fall outflow, determined by the average X2 location, September to December, 1994–2015.

Sources: 20mm Survey, FMWT Survey, and X2 location from Dayflow.

Mechanisms

5. **Delta smelt face many stressors** in the Delta including: degradation of habitat (loss of marshlands and flood plains, and decreasing turbidity), increasing numbers of invasive species (including aquatic weeds which have the potential to alter the ecosystem significantly), increasing predation and competition, increasing loading and toxicity of contaminants, decreasing quantity and quality of food supplies, harmful algal blooms and entrainment. As depicted in the IEP MAST conceptual model, outflow itself does not affect delta smelt directly but hydrology affects delta smelt by interacting with other dynamic drivers to impact landscape and habitat attributes.[15]

Decreasing primary production in the Delta has been well documented (e.g. Jassby et al 2002). Kimmerer (2002a) considered potential mechanisms underlying relationships between the abundance of numerous aquatic organisms and flow. In regards to **food**, he concludes:[16] "For freshwater flow to influence fish and shrimp through the food web would require first that lower trophic levels have positive responses to flow, and that these responses propagate up the food web. **Neither of these mechanisms is supported by the results presented here**." Furthermore "In the Delta, in spring, chlorophyll *a* actually decreased with increasing flow, apparently because of decreasing residence time (Jassby et al. 2002)."[17]

In a detailed analysis of the volume of suitable habitat determined primarily by salinity and flow, Kimmerer et al (2009, p. 12) found that "Despite the evident increase in the amount of habitat, **delta smelt abundance appears to be regulated by other factors so far unidentified**." Feyrer et al (2010) developed a habitat index in the fall comprised of the abiotic elements of temperature, turbidity (Secchi depth) and salinity (electrical conductivity). Importantly, they show graphical relationships[18] where the habitat index increases as outflow increases (X2 decreases), and an increase in abundance as the habitat index increases, thus linking outflow to abundance. Manly et al (2015), in a reanalysis, found the importance of the abiotic elements was reduced when region was considered as a covariate.

Turbidity results from: the transport of suspended sediment during high flow events associated with winter and spring storm events, and sediment resuspension through wind, wave and tidal actions (Schoellhamer et al 2012). While there may be a general relationship between flows and turbidity, artificially increasing flows through reservoir releases may have little influence on turbidity conditions in the delta if sediments have largely settled out in upstream reservoirs. Merely increasing outflows does not provide more inundation of flood plains, nor release more food from them.[19]

Marginal increases in flows have a minimal impact on the dilution of contaminants and may in fact increase the transport of contaminants into the Delta.

The impact of increased flows on introduced species is uncertain. Some studies show that increased flows help various non-native species e.g. striped bass, American shad (Kimmerer et al. 2009).

---

[15] Figure 45, with additional discussion on p.153

[16] p. 48

[17] p. 50

[18] In Figure 2 of their paper

[19] Yolo Bypass, a major floodplain on the Sacramento River system, only flows at significant levels when the Sacramento River reaches a sufficient height to over top the Freemont Weir. Merely releasing additional water from reservoirs would not necessarily create flows in Yolo Bypass. Modifications to Freemont Weir are being considered currently, such that flows in the Bypass may be created at much lower Sacramento River flows.

In trying to resolve uncertainties there have been continuing warnings to focus on cause and effect relationships, and not correlations. For example, an independent scientific review warned: "Many studies—and management decisions—rely on correlations between water flows and fish populations. But the decisions warrant fuller understanding of precisely how the flows affect the fishes."[20] **"Deeper causal understanding is important for identifying and reducing risks to water supply and fish populations."**[21]

While recognizing the correlations between flows and abundance of some species "may be due to several potential mechanisms" Kimmerer (2002b)[22] notes that **"no mechanism has been conclusively shown to underlie the flow relationship of any species"** (in the Delta). He goes on to say: "Several flow-based management actions were established in the mid-1990s, including a salinity standard based on these flow effects, as well as reductions in diversion pumping during critical periods for listed species of fish. **The effectiveness of these actions has not been established.**"

Uncertainty

6. In considering the range of data points in Figures 2, 3, 4 and 5, one can see that numerous data points exist where measures of fish success are high at low outflows, and low at high outflows. Without understanding the underlying mechanisms, it is possible that increasing flows in certain seasons are just as likely to hurt delta smelt as benefit them.

Would the increased outflow achieve the desired results? There is considerable uncertainty about that. Dahm (2016) drawing on Rose et al. (2014) suggests Delta flows are "now largely decoupled from good habitat" (e.g. tidal marshes, floodplains and riparian zones) implying there may be little benefit of more flows if these flows are only going to occur through rip-rapped channels. He does suggest that peak spring flows, access to floodplains and marshes, higher turbidity, and sufficient cool flows in the summer/fall benefit native fishes. Delta water temperature is determined by the interplay between air temperature, flows, winds and tides (Monismith et al. 2009). While water temperatures in summer are primarily affected by air temperatures, an analysis of historical data (see Appendix C) suggests that additional flows in late summer will lower water temperatures in some parts of the Delta. For example, an additional 5,000 cfs of flow in August could lower water temperatures by 0.3 degrees C at Rio Vista.

Regrettably, native species are simply not competing as well as their introduced counterparts (see Figure 6). There has been a significant increase in the abundance of several non-native aquatic species in the Delta. Included among these are: largemouth bass, Mississippi silversides, freshwater Goby and bluegill.

SWRCB decisions protecting water quality and Biological Opinions protecting native fish already ensure that more that 50% of Delta flows are dedicated to outflow. In an average year 18 million acre feet flow out the Delta. Resource managers are faced with the question: will modest increase in flows change the underlying dynamics?

[20] Lund et al. 2015, p.i
[21] Lund et al. 2015, p.i
[22] p. 1275

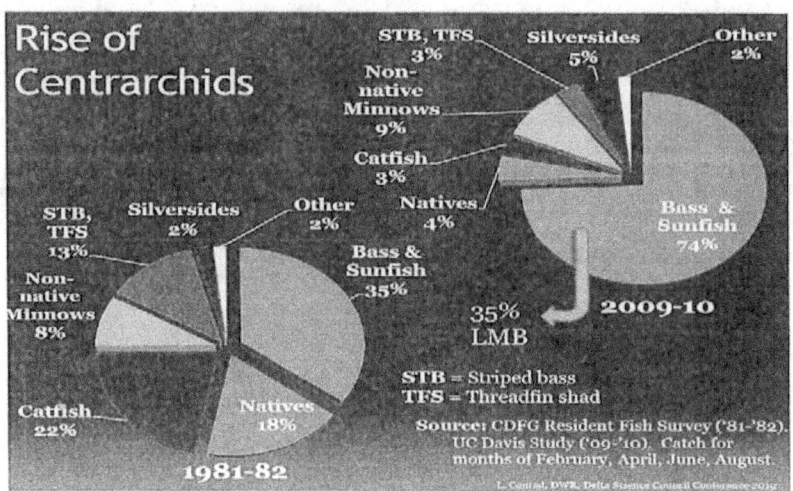

Figure 6. The change in species composition showing native species decreasing from 18% to 4% and bass and sunfish increasing to 74%.

Source: Louse Conrad, DWR.

Water Costs

7. The amount of water required to move X2 varies because the relationship between outflow and X2 is a log-linear relationship. The further west X2 is, the more water it takes to move it another kilometer. Table 1 below shows the amount of water required to move X2 one kilometer west from the monthly average. For the period of February through June, the water cost to move X2 one km is 1.1 million acre feet. Said differently, **the cost to increase the spring abundance index by 1 would be 3.2 million acre feet**. This quantity of water represents a large proportion of the annual supply in the Sacramento valley and is desperately needed for other purposes.

While the percentage increase in outflows will be small, the corresponding percentage change in water supply is much larger. For example, a million acre feet per year represents 7.8% of outflow but 20.4% of exports.[23]

Summary

8. In summary, there is considerable scientific uncertainty surrounding the potential benefits of additional outflow for delta smelt. It appears that:

- increased outflows at any time of the year are unlikely to result in more spawning adults the following winter;
- the underlying mechanisms are yet to be verified;
- the increase will come at an enormous water cost—a challenge for those concerned with a reasonable balancing of beneficial uses; and
- there is a real possibility of potential harm to the species.

In short, there does not appear to be sufficient support at this time for management actions that increase outflows for the purpose of increasing the abundance of delta smelt.

---

[23] Since the implementation of D–1641 in 2000.

Given the uncertainty surrounding the relationship between outflow and the impacts on delta smelt, we would ask that the Collaborative Science and Adaptive Management Program (CSAMP) be asked to consider the issue. Lund et al. (2015) state it well: "Fish abundance is driven by many factors that may or may not be influenced by water flows. The relative contributions of these drivers and the significance of their interactions are inadequately known."[24]

Acknowledgements

This document has benefited from input from numerous reviewers. It remains, however, work in progress and has not yet been subject to independent peer review. Please e-mail comments on this draft to: shamilton@calwatercenter.org

Table 1. Change in X2, and water cost, as a result of increasing outflow by 20%

Month	X2=f(outflow)	R^2	Avg Outflow (cfs)	Change (cfs)	Avg X2 (km)	New X2 (km)	Difference (km)	Water Cost (af)
Jan	y = -9.076 ln(x) + 162.1	0.8141	50,701	10,140	63.77	62.12	1.65	622,404
Feb	y = -9.966 ln(x) + 169.6	0.8015	58,854	11,771	60.15	58.33	1.82	652,568
Mar	y = -10.87 ln(x) + 176.5	0.8876	51,890	10,378	58.49	56.50	1.98	636,997
Apr	y = -10.75 ln(x) + 173.33	0.9089	36,854	7,371	60.30	58.34	1.96	437,823
May	y = -11.48 ln(x) + 179.38	0.9660	25,946	5,189	62.70	60.61	2.09	318,515
Jun	y = -11.64 ln(x) + 182.69	0.9564	15,829	3,166	70.14	68.01	2.12	188,049
Jul	y = 11.46 ln(x) + 181.46	0.8845	8,345	1,669	77.98	75.89	2.09	102,445
Aug	y = -13.25 ln(x) + 195.95	0.9324	6,495	1,299	79.63	77.22	2.42	79,731
Sep	y = -10.25 ln(x) + 173.31	0.8987	8,974	1,795	80.01	78.15	1.87	106,607
Oct	y = 9.758 ln(x) + 169.76	0.8518	9,246	1,849	80.65	78.87	1.78	113,502
Nov	y = -10.90 ln(x) + 178.15	0.8725	13,984	2,797	74.10	72.11	1.99	166,130
Dec	y = -8.554 ln(x) + 158.61	0.7690	30,482	6,096	70.29	68.73	1.56	374,195
Avg or Total							1.94	3,798,967

Source: Dayflow data 1955-2014

The above table and the equations presented in it were derived by fitting a logarithmic function to monthly averages of outflow and X2 location. The resulting water cost estimates are necessarily approximations. Despite the reasonably high goodness of fit coefficients (R^2), the estimates could be refined by employing more precise models such as those employed by Hutton et al (2015). The water cost estimates could also be improved by applying the equations in the second column to the specific year type or flow recommendation, rather than just applying it to an average condition.

---

[24] P.6

Appendix A
Spring Analysis

Regression analysis of the relationship between 20mm Index (dependent variable) and the covariates of Prior Fall Midwater Trawl Index and Feb–Jun X2 for the period 2003–2013.

Year	20mm Index	Prior FMWT Index	Feb-Jun X2
1995	4.4	102	51.4
1996	33.9	899	57.5
1997	19.2	127	63.6
1998	7.7	303	50.2
1999	39.4	420	60.2
2000	23.7	864	62.7
2001	10.9	756	74.0
2002	7.7	603	73.7
2003	13	139	66.7
2004	8.2	210	67.8
2005	15.4	74	63.4
2006	9.8	26	51.3
2007	1	41	75.3
2008	2.9	28	74.8
2009	2.3	23	74.0
2010	3.8	17	67.9
2011	8	29	57.9
2012	11.1	343	73.1
2013	7.8	42	75.0
2014	1.1	18	81.2
2015	0.3	9	80.6

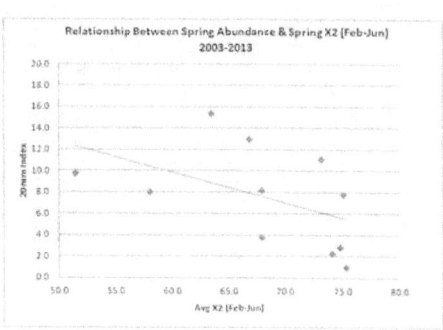

SUMMARY OUTPUT

Dep Var: 20mm Index
Years: 2003-2013 (MAST Report Fiig 79)
Linear Model

Regression Statistics	
Multiple R	0.728
R Square	0.531
Adjusted R Square	0.413
Standard Error	3.559
Observations	11

ANOVA

	df	SS	MS	F	Significance F
Regression	2	114.5126505	57.25633	4.521314	0.048552724
Residual	8	101.3091677	12.66365		
Total	10	215.8218182			

	Coefficients	Standard Error	t Stat	P-value	Lower 95%	Upper 95%
Intercept	28.819	9.859	2.923	0.019	6.083	51.554
Prior FMWT Index	0.025	0.011	2.254	0.054	-0.001	0.050
Feb-Jun X2	-0.345	0.146	-2.362	0.046	-0.682	-0.008

57

Appendix B
Summer Analysis

Regression analysis of the relationship between summer survival (FMWT Index/ STN Index) (dependent variable) and the covariates of Summer Townet Index and Jun–Aug X2 for the period 1995–2015.

Year	FMWT Index	Survival	Jun X2	Jul X2	Aug X2	Avg Jun-Aug X2	STN Index	Trend
1969	313	125.2	55.9	66.6	73.9	65.5	2.5	3
1970	1,673	51.5	79.6	83.3	81.9	81.6	32.5	4
1971	1,303	104.2	66.2	71.5	74.7	70.8	12.5	5
1972	1,265	114.0	85.6	82.4	82.6	83.5	11.1	6
1973	1,145	53.8	76.5	84.1	84.1	81.5	21.3	7
1975	697	57.1	65.1	72.5	76.3	71.3	12.2	9
1976	359	7.1	87.4	87.3	86.6	87.1	50.6	10
1977	480	18.6	93.3	91.8	91.8	92.3	25.8	11
1978	572	9.2	69.7	83.4	85.0	79.4	62.5	12
1980	1,654	104.7	70.1	73.3	81.5	75.0	15.8	14
1981	374	18.9	82.3	84.8	87.3	84.8	19.8	15
1982	333	31.1	60.1	67.2	72.8	66.7	10.7	16
1983	132	45.5	51.7	56.2	63.7	57.2	2.9	17
1984	182	151.7	77.6	77.7	78.4	77.9	1.2	18
1985	110	122.2	82.4	85.8	90.0	86.0	0.9	19
1986	212	26.8	73.5	79.3	82.1	78.3	7.9	20
1987	280	200.0	87.1	88.6	89.9	88.5	1.4	21
1988	174	145.0	88.1	90.0	91.6	89.9	1.2	22
1989	366	166.4	81.0	84.3	83.8	83.0	2.2	23
1990	364	165.5	83.9	87.9	86.4	86.1	2.2	24
1991	689	344.5	87.8	88.8	91.1	89.2	2	25
1992	156	60.0	88.5	91.0	91.1	90.2	2.6	26
1993	1,078	131.5	64.5	73.2	76.3	71.3	8.2	27
1994	102	7.8	84.8	86.2	88.7	86.6	13	28
1995	899	280.9	55.1	61.6	71.2	62.6	3.2	29
1996	127	11.4	65.3	74.7	77.3	72.4	11.1	30
1997	303	75.8	76.6	77.7	77.8	77.4	4	31
1998	420	127.3	53.2	58.9	66.2	59.4	3.3	32
1999	864	72.6	69.8	74.9	79.4	74.7	11.9	33
2000	756	94.5	73.4	77.8	80.0	77.1	8	34
2001	603	172.3	78.5	82.8	87.7	83.0	3.5	35
2002	139	29.6	77.2	81.3	85.1	81.2	4.7	36
2003	210	131.3	69.1	76.7	78.7	74.8	1.6	37
2004	74	25.5	81.2	80.2	82.2	81.2	2.9	38
2005	26	86.7	61.0	71.9	79.9	70.9	0.3	39
2006	41	102.5	56.6	67.9	75.4	66.6	0.4	40
2007	28	70.0	78.6	81.6	86.5	82.3	0.4	41
2008	23	38.3	79.6	84.6	89.3	84.5	0.6	42
2009	17	56.7	76.5	82.0	85.4	81.3	0.3	43
2010	29	36.3	69.1	77.6	83.5	76.8	0.8	44
2011	343	155.9	58.6	64.9	76.2	66.6	2.2	45
2012	42	46.7	77.9	79.4	82.4	79.9	0.9	46
2013	18	25.7	78.3	81.6	83.9	81.2	0.7	47
2014	9	18.0	85.0	85.6	88.1	86.3	0.5	48
2015	7		83.9	85.4	85.5	84.9	0	49

SUMMARY OUTPUT

Dep Variable: FMWT Index/STN Index
Range: 1969-2014 with years ommitted where either index was not available, or zero.

Regression Statistics	
Multiple R	0.470
R Square	0.221
Adjusted R Square	0.162
Standard Error	66.688
Observations	44

ANOVA

	df	SS	MS	F	Significance F
Regression	3	50409	16803	4	0.0177
Residual	40	177894	4447		
Total	43	228303			

	Coefficient	Standard Err	t Stat	P-value	Lower 95%	Upper 95%
Intercept	167.483	96.27	1.74	0.09	-27.09	362.05
Avg Jun-Aug X2	-0.02916	1.20	-0.02	0.98	-2.46	2.41
STN Index	-3.15898	0.95	-3.31	0.00	-5.09	-1.23
Trend	-1.85312	0.92	-2.02	0.05	-3.71	0.00

Appendix C
Analysis of Factors Affecting Water Temperature

Regression analysis of the relationship between average monthly water temperatures at Rio Vista (dependent variable) and the covariates of 15 day average air temperature at Davis, Ca, and flows at Rio Vista during the period 1983–2014.

	One Std Dev		Resulting Change in Water Temp at Rio Vista due to a 1 std dev change in:		R^2	t Statistics	
Month	15 Day Avg Air Temp	Rio Vista Flows	15 Day Avg Air Temp	Flows at Rio Vista		Davis Air Temp	Rio Vista Flows
	°C	(cfs)	°C	°C			
Jan	1.79	18,738	0.96	0.17	0.64	36.42	6.49
Feb	1.64	18,104	1.18	-0.06	0.72	44.89	-2.25
Mar	2.03	16,468	1.31	-0.47	0.73	41.45	-14.80
Apr	1.87	15,984	0.99	-0.69	0.71	28.31	-19.68
May	2.30	17,523	1.18	-1.00	0.79	38.14	-32.39
Jun	2.02	12,967	0.83	-0.99	0.74	27.50	-32.91
Jul	1.49	6,698	0.69	-0.54	0.49	22.63	-17.66
Aug	1.40	5,212	0.42	-0.28	0.35	19.08	-13.52
Sep	1.72	6,076	0.81	-0.47	0.59	31.17	-17.93
Oct	2.21	6,474	1.31	-0.29	0.72	47.28	-10.58
Nov	2.39	8,962	1.58	-0.28	0.85	61.54	-10.82
Dec	2.00	15,965	1.33	-0.04	0.73	48.95	-1.58

The second and third columns are the calculated standard deviations for 15-day average air temperature at Davis, in degrees Celsius, and Rio Vista flows, in cfs, by month. The third and fourth columns show the change is water temperature at Rio Vista resulting from the one standard deviation change shown in columns two and three. These equations were estimated using ordinary least squares regression, with flows being converted to log form. The regression coefficient and t-statistics are reported in the last three columns. Note that the explanatory power of these covariates varies by month, from a high in November to a low in August, suggesting that additional factors are important in late summer. The consequence of a one standard deviation increase in flows at Rio Vista varies from of a 1.0 degree decrease in water temperature in May to a one 0.17 degree increase in January. The temperature impacts are expected to become more muted the further west temperatures are examined as water temperatures become more influenced by tides.

There are more sophisticated and elegant treatments of the factors affecting water temperature in the Delta (e.g. Monismith et al 2009). The purpose of the above analysis was to distinguish the influence of flows and air temperature.

References

Dahm, C. (2016) "Delta Stewardship Council, Delta Science Program," Presentation to the SWRCB, April, 2016.

EET (1996) An assessment of the Likely Mechanism Underlying the "Fish-X2" Relationships, Draft, Interagency Ecological Program, Estuarine Ecology Team, June 1996. http://www.iep.water.ca.gov/eet/x2fish.html, Downloaded 9/2/2008.

Feyrer, F., Nobriga, M., and Sommer, T. (2007) Multi-decadal trends for three declining fish species: habitat patterns and mechanisms in the San Francisco Estuary, California, U.S.A. Canadian Journal of Fisheries and Aquatic Sciences 64:723–734.

Feyrer, F., Newman, K., Nobriga, M., and Sommer, T. (2011) Modeling the effects of future outflow on the abiotic habitat of an imperiled estuarine fish. Estuaries and Coasts 34:120–128. doi:10.1007/s12237-010-9343-9. Available at: http://caestuaries.opennrm.org/assets/46ab8c3f52c799c8f3ab3f2f514bd145/application/pdf/Feyrer_et_al.2011.pdf

Jassby, A., Kimmerer, W.J., Monismith, S.G., Armor, C., Cloern, J.E., Powell, T.M., Schubel, J.R., and Vendlinski, T.J. (1995) Isohaline position as a habitat indicator for estuarine populations. Ecological Applications 5:272–289.

Jassby, A.D., Cloern, J.E., Cole, B.E. (2002) Annual primary production: patterns and mechanisms of change in a nutrient rich tidal estuary. Limnol Oceanogr 47(3):698–712.

Hutton, P.H., Rath, J.S., Chen, L., Ungs, M.J., and Roy, S.B. (2015) Nine decades of salinity observations in the San Francisco Bay and Delta: Modeling and Trend Evaluations, Journal of Water Resources Planning & Management, 142(3). Available at: http://ascelibrary.org/doi/abs/10.1061/(ASCE)WR.1943-5452.0000617

Kimmerer, W.J., Gross, E.S., and MacWilliams, M.L. (2009) Is the response of estuarine nekton to freshwater flow in the San Francisco estuary explained by variation in habitat volume? Estuaries and Coasts. 32:375–389. Available at: http://www.springerlink.com/content/26pr3h5574605083/

Kimmerer, W.J. (2002a) Effects of freshwater flow on abundance of estuarine organisms: physical effects or trophic linkages? Marine Ecology Progress Series 243:39–55. Available at: http://www.waterrights.ca.gov/baydelta/docs/exhibits/DOI-EXH-331.pdf

Kimmerer, W.J. (2002b) Physical, biological, and management responses to variable freshwater flow into the San Francisco Estuary. Estuaries 25:1275–1290. Available at: http://www.springerlink.com/content/184496u50723t617/fulltext.pdf

IEP MAST (2015) An updated conceptual model of Delta Smelt biology: our evolving understanding of an estuarine fish, Interagency Ecological Program, Management, Analysis and Synthesis Team. Technical Report 90. Available at: http://water.ca.gov/iep/docs/Delta_Smelt_MAST_Synthesis_Report_January%202015.pdf

Lund, J., et al (2015) Flows and Fishes in the Sacramento-San Joaquin Delta: Research needs in support of adaptive management—A review by the Delta Independent Science Board. Available at: http://deltacouncil.ca.gov/sites/default/files/2015/09/2015-9-29-15-0929-Final-Fishes-and-Flows-in-the-Delta.pdf

MacNally, R., Thomson, J.R., Kimmerer, W.J., Feyrer, F., Newman, K.B., Andy Sih, A., Bennett, W.A., Brown, L., Fleishman, E., Culberson, S.D., and Castillo, G. (2010) Analysis of pelagic species decline in the upper San Francisco Estuary using multivariate autoregressive modelling (MAR), Ecological Applications 20:1417–1430. Available online at: http://online.sfsu.edu/modelds/Files/References/MacNallyetal2010EcoApps.pdf

Manly, B.F.J., Fullerton, D., Hendrix, A.N., and Burnham, K.P. (2015) Comments on Feyrer et al. "Modeling the Effects of Future Outflow on the Abiotic Habitat of an Imperiled Estuarine Fish," Estuaries and Coasts 38:1815–1820. DOI 10.1007/s12237-014-9905-3

Monismith, S.G., J.L. Hench, D.A. Fong, N.J. Nidzieko, W.E. Fleenor, L.P. Doyle, and S.G. Schladow. (2009) Thermal variability in a tidal river. Estuaries and Coasts 32:100–110. Available at: http://www.centerforoceansolutions.org/sites/default/files/publications/Monismith_et_al_2009_ESTUARIES.pdf

Nobriga, M.L., Sommer, T.R., Feyer, F., and Fleming, K. (2008) Long-Term Trends in Summertime Habitat Suitability for Delta Smelt, *Hypomesus transpacificus*, San Francisco Estuary and Watershed Science 6(1). Available at: http://eprints.cdlib.org/uc/item/5xd3q8tx

Rose et al (2014) Delta Interior Inflows and Related Stressors, Presentation by the Independent Science Board, July 25, 2014. Available at: http://deltacouncil.ca.gov/sites/default/files/documents/files/Item_9_Kenneth_Rose_Presentation.pdf

Schoellhamer, D.H., Wright, S.A., and Drexler, J.Z. (2012) Conceptual model of sedimentation in the Sacramento-San Joaquin River Delta. San Francisco Estuary and Watershed Science 10(3). Available at: http://www.escholarship.org/uc/item/2652z8sq

Thomson, J.R., Kimmerer, W.J., Brown, L.R., Newman, K.B., MacNally, R., Bennett, W.A., Feyrer, F., and Fleishman, E. (2009) Bayesian change-point analysis of abundance trends for pelagic fishes in the upper San Francisco Estuary. Ecological Applications 20:1431–1448. Available online at: http://online.sfsu.edu/modelds/Files/References/ThomsonEtal2010EcoApps.pdf

––––––––

Mr. LAMALFA. Thank you for your indulgence, sir.

Dr. FLEMING. Mrs. Lummis.

Mrs. LUMMIS. Thank you, Mr. Chairman.

You may be wondering why a Member from Wyoming would come to a hearing that is mostly a coastal states' issue. I got to go to Fresno to a hearing on the Delta smelt, and I got to see the dried up almond trees, the dead pistachio trees. We got to meet the farmers who are out of work, both owners and workers who are desperately trying to hang on to a culture, a way of life, a community. And they came together to address these issues, and it was kind of moving. So, I continue to have an interest in this issue.

My question is for you, and I am going to need help with your name. Is it Murillo, Mr. Murillo?

Mr. MURILLO. Yes.

Mrs. LUMMIS. OK. And I can address this also to your colleagues at the Department of the Interior. How do two different agencies who are overseeing endangered species act in contradiction to each other? We have Fish and Wildlife Service and NMFS, each in a tug-of-war. One wants more flow, the other wants less. They seem to be operating in a vacuum. Why shouldn't there be one biological opinion that covers both the smelt and the salmon?

Mr. MURILLO. That would be optimal if we could have one biological opinion. And hopefully, we can get there some day. But with respect to the tug-of-war, what we do, like we do in normal years, there are a lot of competing demands in the system, just like there was this year. What we did is we brought the directors together, Fish and Wildlife and NMFS together, and myself, and we worked up a temperature plan that would not only meet the NOAA requirements, but also leave some flexibility so that we could provide the outflows for the Delta smelt.

Mrs. LUMMIS. Gentlemen—and I am sorry, I just walked in so I am a little behind the curve—could you also address that? NMFS and Fish and Wildlife are both represented here, correct?

Oh, great. Could you enlighten me?

Dr. LOHOEFENER. Sure. I will try. I am Ren Lohoefener, Regional Director for the Fish and Wildlife Service.

Actually, we tried that prior to 2008. We were under court orders, both National Marine Fish Reserves and Fish and Wildlife Service, to deliver opinions. Those court orders, unfortunately, did not allow us the time to mesh those opinions into one. I think both my colleague from NOAA Fisheries would agree, ideally, we will have one coordinated biological opinion. I hope that is the future.

Mrs. LUMMIS. And you can respond to this additional question. Is the court's decision binding upon you in perpetuity?

Mr. LOHOEFENER. No, we are no longer under that opinion. As Congressman Huffman pointed out, those opinions have been reviewed and found to be valid. There is nothing that keeps us in the future from doing a coordinated single opinion.

Mrs. LUMMIS. OK.

Mr. COSTA. Would the gentlewoman yield?

Mrs. LUMMIS. Yes.

Mr. COSTA. Before you came in, I asked a question and Mr. Lohoefener responded, on the summer outflow, was this a part of the biological opinion or not? And he responded by saying that no, it is not part of the biological opinion. So I think it is important to note that. And the Bureau of Reclamation indicated this was a voluntary action that they were taking.

Mrs. LUMMIS. Oh. So reclaiming my time, as I understand it, there has been a decline from 10,500 cfs to 8,000 cfs. Why?

Mr. MURILLO. The proposal was to have a plan where we release 8,000 cfs. The final plan ends up with a July release of 10,500.

Mrs. LUMMIS. Thank you.

I do want to double back to the gentleman from NMFS.

Mr. THOM. Yes. Thank you. I would just second that. I think in terms of dealing with the changing circumstances in May where the scientists, in terms of temperature profiling, realized there was less cold water in Shasta Reservoir for fish, the Bureau came back to us to revise the plan so that we could maintain temperature criteria. I just want to point out that Mr. Murillo, Mr. Lohoefener, and myself worked together with our staff to come to a plan that actually merged the benefits to smelt and salmon in the system to come up with a plan that would actually work and reach agreement and move us forward this year.

So, I think that has been a success of the agencies working together to get a plan that can actually operate through this year and help protect winter-run fish in the river.

Mrs. LUMMIS. Thank you.

My time is about to expire, so I yield back.

Dr. FLEMING. The gentlelady yields.

Mr. Denham.

Mr. DENHAM. Thank you, Mr. Chairman.

Mr. Murillo, you and I have worked together quite a bit on water deliveries and movement throughout the Central Valley. I want to see if you can give me an update on New Melones and the increased storage that we could possibly have there.

Mr. MURILLO. I don't have the details on New Melones right now. I know that that part of the system is drier than it has been in the past. But I don't have any update on that. I apologize.

Mr. DENHAM. OK. If you could get back to me on that. I know it is an issue that we have talked about in the past.

Mr. MURILLO. Absolutely.

Mr. DENHAM. I wanted to follow up on predation. At the April 20 hearing, Mr. LaMalfa talked about predation, what the Federal agencies have done already and what is being proposed from the Federal agencies. What we got back was from the Administration to fulfill an action required by the 2009 BiOp, they are basically talking about capturing and relocating striped bass.

Is the capture and relocation of the striped bass so that they don't eat anywhere from 93 to 98 percent of the salmon we are trying to save? First of all, do you agree with the relocation? And if not, what else would you propose?

Mr. Sutton, let's start with you. I would just ask for a quick response so I can get to everybody.

Mr. SUTTON. Predation is a huge issue that is working against everything we are doing, and it is a stressor that needs serious and immediate attention.

Mr. DENHAM. Thank you.

Mr. Murillo?

Mr. MURILLO. Yes. Predation, as we mentioned, is something we do have to address. Whether we relocate the bass or not, I am not sure what the benefit of that is, so I will leave that up to the fisheries to maybe comment on that.

Mr. DENHAM. Thank you.

Mr. THOM. OK. And I would just add, Mr. Denham, we have been supportive of predation efforts. We had this conversation before. We are studying it, we are looking at hot spots. I think predator removal, predator relocation, and getting the predators out of these hot spots has been shown to be effective. But there is ongoing research about the predator effects throughout the system and other methods that might be able to be taken to deal with them as well.

Mr. DENHAM. Thank you.

Mr. Borck?

Mr. BORCK. I don't like invasive species, but I don't believe that removing a single predator would fix a problem as big as this. There are a lot of other predators out there. I don't see it as a panacea. You can take the creel limits off and let sportsmen catch all you want. I don't think that would fix it.

Mr. DENHAM. Thank you.

Mr. Azhderian?

Mr. AZHDERIAN. I do think that addressing hot spots is certainly the right place to start. Dr. Hayes, with the National Marine Fisheries Service, has done a lot of that research. I think would agree with that conclusion.

I think the part that is most frustrating for us, though, is that there is a great deal of uncertainty about standards in the biological opinions that affect the rate of pumping, and those are imposed with great vigor. When we are sitting down and talking about other stressors such as predation, the response is often, "Well, we are not sure, so we are going to study it." So, it is sort of the disproportionate response to the problem that I think we struggle with quite often.

Mr. DENHAM. Thank you.

And just to follow up, Mr. Borck, I am a little bit surprised by your answer. Obviously, I don't think this is a panacea either. I think we actually need more storage. The storage would solve a lot of our problems. But if 98 percent of the fish are getting—the fish that you want to fish, the 23,000 jobs that you want to make sure we still have, if 98 percent of the fish are getting eaten by non-native species, isn't any type of help—I mean, if we could save an extra 3, 4 percent, doesn't that help your business?

Mr. BORCK. Like I said, I am fine with the concept of taking the creel limits off and allowing sports fishermen to catch all the stripers they want. I just don't see it having that big an impact ultimately. Unfortunately, if you take stripers out, then shad get bigger, shad can eat salmon when they are as small as a guppy. So we may just be trading one predator for another. So, I don't see it as a good enough fix to key in on it.

Mr. DENHAM. I don't see it as a good enough fix either, but I certainly see a doubling goal of the fish that—if you are doubling the amount of fish that are eating all of the threatened and endangered species, that might not be the best policy for our Federal Government to take.

I yield back the rest of my time.

Dr. FLEMING. The gentleman yields.

Mr. Newhouse.

Mr. NEWHOUSE. Thank you, Mr. Chairman. Thank you all for being here this morning.

Being from the state of Washington, I am somewhat reluctant to get engaged in this California water war. I am like Mr. Costa, it is easy to let it drive you crazy. But if it weren't so important to not only the economy, but also the food supply of our whole country, as well as how you solve, or how we help you solve, your water issues will greatly impact how we solve water issues in the Pacific Northwest as well. So, this is a big issue.

I heard from Mr. LaMalfa in his opening comments some frustration about contrary policy by different agencies in the basin, or in the state. I think I heard that there were competing biological opinions and some interest in connecting those or making them into one, if that is a possibility.

Mr. Azhderian, you also expressed some frustration associated with a lack of transparency and collaboration. From those of us from the outside looking in, these California water wars have been going on for a long time. There must be a better way. And I think maybe we have touched on some of those avenues of doing this better, the collaboration, the transparency, all looking toward a similar goal of increased water availability, returning fish populations, habitat, but also protecting our very important agricultural industry and fishing industry.

So what would a better model look like? All of you from different perspectives. I will start with you, Mr. Azhderian.

Mr. AZHDERIAN. Yes, I think a better model is one that is inclusive. The Federal agencies have talked about improved collaboration among them. And I do believe that that is true. I think Reclamation, in particular, has done its level best to try and communicate outcomes to users of CVP water. But communicating outcomes is something very different than actually collaborating on solutions.

So, I think broadening the inclusion in the questions and testing hypotheses, developing solutions, and using the unique abilities of water agencies, in particular, to solve the problems is really an asset that we have underutilized, a great tool moving forward. Moving away from the common processes where we are relying strictly on statistical analyses, or largely on that, and getting into doing the research and understanding what the underlying biological factors are, is another essential key if we are going to make our water management and our environmental management actions more efficient and more effective. After all, what we are all interested in is effective environmental protection.

There are a lot of tools that are out there, there are models from the Bay Delta Accord as far back as the early 1990s, all the way to recently with the Delta Reform Act that talk about the importance of comprehensive solutions and inclusive collaborations. And there are several recommendations from a number of science panels as well about how that can be achieved. There are minds greater than mine that have commented on this. There is a wealth of information, we just need to start using it.

Mr. NEWHOUSE. Real quickly, could I ask the fisherman, Mr. Borck, and I will go to our farmer as well. And then if there is time, hopefully from the agencies.

Mr. BORCK. The quick answer is I am a harvester. I have to leave modeling and those kind of situations to scientists, guys with Ph.D.'s. My trust has always been in the best available science.

Mr. NEWHOUSE. OK. I appreciate that.

Mr. Sutton.

Mr. SUTTON. Similar answer. A more robust process is needed to ensure those regulatory actions are informed by sound science and there is accountability and a measure to achieving outcomes. There is a model we can follow just within David's region at Klamath where they spent 2 years on a collaborative process bringing in all the stakeholders to form a VA and resulted in one biological opinion. In my opinion, that effort is something we need to focus on.

Mr. NEWHOUSE. And then, Mr. Murillo, if you could speak for the Federal Government, where can Congress help?

Mr. MURILLO. Well, I agree with the statements made here today that we try to be transparent. We can be more inclusive, but inclusive means not just including the Ag. community, we also have to include the environmental groups, the tribes, and the power users, bringing them all together. So I think, as we move forward, that is something that we will try to improve on.

Mr. NEWHOUSE. Well, it is not going to get any easier with California's population expected to double in the next 25 years or so.

Mr. MURILLO. It is getting bigger.

Mr. NEWHOUSE. Yes, so we have a problem that we have to solve.

Mr. MURILLO. Absolutely.

Mr. NEWHOUSE. Thank you.

Thank you, Mr. Chairman.

Dr. FLEMING. OK. We thank the witnesses for your valuable testimony today. Members of the subcommittee may have additional questions for witnesses. We ask you to respond to these in writing. The hearing record will be open for 10 days to receive these responses.

Again, I would like to thank our staff. The preparation for a hearing like this can take many hours, 40 or more hours, and it is a lot of work. So, we appreciate our staff and all the great work they do. I will certainly cite Kiel, in particular, as being a real leader in all of this. We thank Kiel for that.

So, if there is no further business, without objection, the subcommittee stands adjourned.

[Whereupon, at 11:24 a.m., the subcommittee was adjourned.]

○